THE WALLACE COLLECTION

The Wallace Collection,
Hertford House

2

John Ingamells

The Wallace Collection

SCALA BOOKS

© 1990 The Wallace Collection

First published in 1990 by
Scala Publications Ltd
3 Greek Street
London W1V 6NX

ISBN 1 870248 47 3

Designed by Alan Bartram
Edited by Paul Holberton
Produced by Scala Publications
Filmset by August Filmsetting, St Helens, England
Printed and bound by Graphicom, Vicenza, Italy

FRONT COVER
The Swing (detail). Jean-Honoré Fragonard. 1767

BACK COVER
The 'Laughing Cavalier'. Frans Hals. 1624

Contents

The fourth Marquess of Hertford
(left) with Mme Oger and his son
Richard Wallace at Bagatelle, *c*1860

The Wallace Collection

The Wallace Collection was bequeathed to the British nation by Lady Wallace in 1897, and was opened to the public as a national museum three years later. Lady Wallace was the widow of Sir Richard Wallace, the illegitimate son of Richard Seymour-Conway, fourth Marquess of Hertford, and the Collection had been accumulated principally by successive Marquesses of Hertford, though their contributions were unequal. According to the Founder's Deed of Trust, the Wallace Collection is 'kept together, unmixed with other objects of art', which means that nothing may be added to it, nor any loan be made or received. This wise provision has preserved the remarkable character of one of the greatest collections ever made by an English family. The illustrations in this book suggest the range and quality of the Collection, and the essay which follows briefly outlines its history.

The story begins with Francis Seymour-Conway (1719-94), created first Marquess of Hertford in 1793, just before his death. He could claim descent from Edward Seymour, first Earl of Hertford, Lord Protector of England from 1547 to 1549. A loyal Tory, the first Marquess followed a successful diplomatic career, his appointments including those of Ambassador in Paris (1762-65) and Lord Chamberlain (1766-92). He was not a dedicated collector, but he occasionally bought pictures for both his country seat, Ragley Hall in Warwickshire (which remains the seat of the Marquesses of Hertford), and his town house in Grosvenor Street; of these six Canalettos are now in the Wallace Collection. He also owned Sudbourn Hall in Suffolk, Conway Castle in Wales and estates in Lisburn, near Belfast.

His eldest son, Francis, second Marquess of Hertford (1743-1822), followed a similar career, being Ambassador in Berlin and Vienna (1793-94) and Lord Chamberlain (1812-21). In 1797 he acquired the lease of Hertford House, now the home of the Wallace Collection, then situated on the outskirts of London in a wooded area renowned for its duck-shooting. He was married twice, each time to a rich heiress who duly enhanced the family's considerable fortunes, the second time to Isabella, daughter of Lord Irwin of Temple Newsam. Between 1807 and 1818 she became the *confidante* of the Prince of Wales, later Prince Regent and finally George IV, whose infatuation attracted considerable comment. The liaison is commemorated in the Wallace Collection by Gainsborough's portrait of Mary 'Perdita' Robinson, the Prince's first mistress, which he gave, perhaps a little tactlessly, to the second Marquess in 1818. By that time the Marquess had already purchased other good English portraits, such as the *Nelly O'Brien* by Reynolds, although, like his father, he appears to have been a casual purchaser of works of art. On the death of his Marchioness in 1834 Hertford House contained a number of English portraits, French Boulle furniture, furnishing bronzes and some Sèvres porcelain, some items of which can be identified today in the Wallace Collection.

Their only surviving child, Francis, third Marquess of Hertford (1777-1842), was the first real collector in the family. A restive, rather disreputable character, he married, against his parents' wishes and as soon as he came of age in 1798, Maria Fagnani, the daughter of an Italian *marchesa* and either the fourth Duke of Queensberry ('Old Q') or George Selwyn, both of whom left her large sums of money and properties in central London in the belief that they were her father.

Manchester House, later Hertford
House, 1813

Their legacies further increased the family's already considerable wealth. Though their son Richard was born in 1800, the marriage was not a success. By 1803 the Marchioness was living on her own in some style in Paris, where she bore a second, illegitimate, son, Lord Henry Seymour (1805-59), and where she died in 1856. The Marquess led an increasingly dissipated existence in London and travelled regularly on the Continent. He had been a close friend of the Prince of Wales whose devotion to the second Marchioness has been mentioned; both gave much time to the pursuit of pleasure, and both exercised remarkable taste in the collection of works of art. Lord Hertford would study old sale catalogues and attend to the condition and pedigree of the pictures he bought. He was particularly knowledgeable concerning Dutch paintings and many of his discerning purchases are to be seen in the Wallace Collection, while the Royal Collection has many more which he bought for the Prince (the best known being Rembrandt's *Shipbuilder and his wife*). In turn the Prince encouraged Lord Hertford to acquire French eighteenth-century furniture, Italianate bronzes and Sèvres porcelain, such as he was himself collecting for his new, but short-lived residence, Carlton House. Their friendship had cooled by 1820 when the Prince acceded as George IV, and Lord Hertford's activity as a collector was then almost over. His London houses, St Dunstan's Villa in Regent's Park and Dorchester House in Park Lane, were richly furnished. Crimson carpets and curtains set off his Boulle furniture and objects of art, while his Dutch pictures were mixed with older portraits and some Italian paintings. There was a remarkable collection of miniatures in Dorchester House 'of at least half a hundred lovely women, black, brown, fair and even carrotty', and in the Bow Room of the same house hung Titian's *Perseus and Andromeda* which, although an exceptional purchase for the third Marquess, has become perhaps his best known. It is now possible to respect his achievement as a collector, but when he died a contemporary alleged that 'no man ever lived more despised or died less regretted'.

His only son, Richard, fourth Marquess of Hertford (1800-70), was the greatest collector in the family. His neurotic diffidence contrasted with his father's ebullience. Intelligent and sensitive, he succeeded to a vast fortune and could have exerted considerable political influence, to the extent that he was considered by some a future Tory Prime Minister. Yet by the time he was thirty, after having been briefly an officer in the Hussars, an attaché at the Embassies in Constantinople and Paris, and a Tory MP for Lisburn, he had renounced any public rôle. His Irish estates lay neglected as he settled in Paris in the rue Laffitte, near his adored mother, and acquired the charming château of Bagatelle in the Bois de Boulogne as a country retreat. He was known in Parisian society, and became the intimate friend of the Emperor, Napoleon III. Yet, despite such advantages, he lived, as an acquaintance later expressed it, 'a withdrawn, invisible life, always seeming to be ill, only opening his door to a chosen few and, since he was absolutely indifferent to all movement and life, would not even have drawn back his curtains to see a revolution go by in the street below'.

It was only as a collector that the fourth Marquess seemed to find any form of fulfilment. Between 1840 and 1870 he bought paintings, French eighteenth-century furniture, sculpture, tapestries, porcelain, miniatures, and Oriental arms and

1

2

1
The third Marquess of Hertford,
*c*1824
Henry Bone after Thomas
Lawrence, enamel, 10 × 7.5 cm
(MA3)

2
The fourth Marquess of Hertford,
*c*1855

3
Bagatelle, Bois de Boulogne, Paris,
*c*1860

4
The rue Laffitte running into the
boulevard des Italiens, Paris,
showing the rotunda of Lord
Hertford's apartments at 2 rue
Laffitte

3

4

Sir Richard Wallace in Hertford
House, 1888

Lady Wallace, *c*1890

armour. Unlike his father, he did not buy just to furnish his rooms; he accumulated on a grand scale. It has been said that more than a hundred French clocks eventually stood in the rue Laffitte, where the picture gallery boasted an almost reckless hang: Velázquez, Boucher, Hals and Hobbema hung side by side, while nineteenth-century French histories and landscapes surrounded Dutch still lifes and seventeenth-century French portraits. In Hertford House, which he rarely visited, many of the purchases he made in the London sale-rooms through his agents remained for long periods in their packing cases, a circumstance which concerned a visiting German art-historian, Dr Waagen. 'Old pictures require perpetual vigilance', he wrote; 'it is much to be feared that, after having remained packed for many years, excluded from light and air, they will be found on opening the cases in a more or less injured condition.' Lord Hertford's principal London agent, Samuel Mawson, eventually put matters right, but the episode strongly suggests that for Lord Hertford acquisition was everything, and counted for far more than display — an attitude entirely consistent with his character.

Although his purchases included many quite outstanding seventeenth-century paintings (as the illustrations here show), Lord Hertford was known particularly as a collector of French eighteenth-century art. Perhaps he recognised the parallel between his own privileged position in society and that of the nobility of the *ancien régime*. Like them, he loved 'pleasing' subjects in his pictures, and delighted in the finest craftsmanship. By the end of his life he had, for example, 32 paintings by Boucher, 26 by Greuze, and 42 by Watteau and his pupils Lancret and Pater. No other Englishman was then seriously collecting such pictures and, to this day, the French eighteenth-century paintings in the Wallace Collection remain without compare in Britain. With furniture Lord Hertford particularly prized those fine pieces which had belonged to the French Crown before the Revolution, of which the chest of drawers made by Gaudreaus for Louis XV in 1739 and the drop-front writing desk (secretaire) made by Riesener in 1780 for Marie-Antoinette are outstanding examples.

Lord Hertford died at Bagatelle on 24 August 1870, as the Prussian army approached Paris and nine days before Napoleon III's surrender at Sedan. He had not married but, by one Mrs Agnes Jackson, née Wallace, he had an illegitimate son born in London in 1818 who had been brought up in Paris by the third Marchioness. The boy became his father's agent and secretary and then, somewhat unexpectedly, his heir. He could not, of course, inherit the Marquisate which passed to a cousin, nor any entailed items in the family's collection, but he inherited the Paris properties and his father's wonderful collection; he also received the Irish estates, Sudbourn Hall and the lease of Hertford House. Sir Richard Wallace (1818-90), born Richard Jackson, had changed his surname in 1842 to his mother's maiden name, and from such obscurity the Wallace Collection derives its name. On his inheritance Wallace resolved, it would appear, to redeem the indifference his father and grandfather had shown to their fellow-men. During the Prussian siege of Paris and the ensuing civil strife of the Commune in 1870-71, he furnished the beleaguered citizens, both English and French, with welfare funds and medical facilities on a lavish scale, and for such beneficence Queen Victoria made him a

1
Hertford House: the Long Picture
Gallery (now gallery 19), *c*1890

2
Hertford House: the European
Armoury (now gallery 20), *c*1890

Baronet in 1872. The previous year Wallace had married Julie Castelnau, his long-time companion and the mother of his thirty-year-old son.

In 1872 Wallace decided to settle in Hertford House. He brought over from Paris as much of his collection as he could, adding it to the comparatively small family collection which was already there. Between 1872 and 1875 he allowed these collections to be exhibited at the new Bethnal Green Museum, while Hertford House was extended and modified to accommodate his treasures. Meantime he extended the historical scope of the collections by acquiring a number of medieval and Renaissance works of art, including a fine collection of European arms and armour. Most of these objects came from two French private collections formed during the Second Empire and now offered for sale by their dispossessed or apprehensive owners, the comte de Nieuwerkerke, Napoleon III's Minister of Fine Arts, and the vicomte de Tauzia, a Keeper of Drawings at the Louvre. There may have been an element of charity in Wallace's purchases, but he had previously shown his interest in what was then called 'primitive' art in a small collection he had assembled as a young man and sold off in 1857. When all Wallace's works of art were finally installed in the restyled Hertford House in 1875 they formed an incomparable private collection.

Although Wallace conscientiously fulfilled a number of public rôles, serving as Tory MP for Lisburn, and as a Trustee of the National Galleries in London and Dublin, and though he was able to entertain the Prince of Wales at Sudbourn and was both admired and respected by his tenants and constituents, yet he seems not to have found any great happiness in his new life. Following the death of his son in 1887, he returned alone to Bagatelle where he died, in the same room as his father, in 1890.

Lady Wallace (1819-97), a perfume-seller in Paris when Wallace first met her, had not coped very well with the rôle of an English Lady. She spoke no English and her appearance latterly was not prepossessing. But it fell to her to bequeath her husband's collection at Hertford House to the British nation, doubtless according to Wallace's instructions. There remained, of course, much more of Wallace's inherited collection in Paris, particularly French eighteenth-century sculpture, furniture and tapestries. These, together with the Paris properties, passed to Lady Wallace's residuary legatee, Sir John Murray Scott (1847-1912), who had previously been secretary to Sir Richard and Lady Wallace. He became a Trustee of The Wallace Collection and played an important part in the conversion of Hertford House into a public museum. He died from heart failure on the Board Room table then in gallery 9. He had already sold Bagatelle to the City of Paris and he bequeathed all his inherited works of art to Lady Sackville of Knole, of whom he was somewhat enamoured. Lady Sackville immediately sold everything to a Parisian dealer who, over the next twenty years, dispersed these treasures, principally to American collectors.

The story of the Wallace Collection reads at times like fiction, yet it was in such improbable circumstances that it was formed. It remains the noblest achievement of five generations of a quite extraordinary family.

Medieval and Renaissance

The richness of these medieval and Renaissance collections has often been overlooked, yet they provide a remarkable survey of an intriguing aspect of nineteenth-century taste and contain several individual masterpieces. Their presence is due almost entirely to Sir Richard Wallace who acquired the majority of these works of art between 1871 and 1875, after he had inherited his father's extraordinary collection of seventeenth- to nineteenth-century works of art. Earlier in his life he had formed a collection which his father had made him sell in Paris in 1857 to offset the serious consequences of rash speculations at the Bourse. That sale catalogue already revealed the antiquarian streak in Wallace; it included maiolica, glass, Renaissance bronzes and ivories, as well as later works of art in his father's taste. When he suddenly became a very rich man and the owner of one of Europe's most famous collections, he revived these antiquarian instincts to extend its historical scope. His father had bought, late in his life, the fine bronze bust by Pilon of *Charles IX* and the beautiful Renaissance bronze of a *Seated nymph* by Giovanni da Crema, but these were isolated and uncharacteristic purchases.

Wallace acted quickly and on a grand scale, purchasing two collections of medieval and Renaissance works of art formed in France during the Second Empire, the larger by the comte de Nieuwerkerke who had been Napoleon III's flamboyant Minister of Fine Arts, the smaller by the vicomte de Tauzia, the knowledgeable Assistant Keeper of Paintings and Drawings in the Louvre. Both Nieuwerkerke and Tauzia had decided to sell following the disturbances of the Franco-Prussian War and the ensuing terror of the Commune. Nieuwerkerke had then left France disguised as a valet, and his fortunes only revived when Wallace purchased his collection in 1871, enabling him to start a new life in Italy. Tauzia, though he retained and improved his position at the Louvre, sold his collection to Wallace in Paris in 1872. Wallace bought a number of individual items in the earlier 1870s, such as the fine Gubbio maiolica dish with the bathing maidens (C66), the Urbino maiolica wine cooler (C107), a beautiful enamel diptych (XII A68) and a curious sixteenth-century wax diptych (S417), but by far the greater part of his medieval and Renaissance collection came from Nieuwerkerke and Tauzia.

The taste for such medieval and Renaissance art had grown up with the nineteenth century. The awakening of an interest in the past had been popularly expressed in the novels of Scott and Dumas, while on a more serious level the magnificent Sommerard collection of medieval and Renaissance antiquities, installed in the hôtel de Cluny in Paris in 1832, was opened as the Musée de Cluny in 1844. In the 1850s and more particularly in the 1860s, Nieuwerkerke greedily acquired such *objets*. His armoury is discussed in the following section, but here one may point, for example, to his outstanding pieces of Italian maiolica (C27) and Limoges enamel (III F253), Venetian and *façon de Venise* glass (XXV B96, III E174), Renaissance sculpture, including the astonishing boxwood *Hercules* (S273), ivories (S249) and other *curiosités*, such as rock-crystal figures and wax portraits. It was the taste of an amateur enthusiast responding to a new fashion, becoming more knowledgeable with time, though proving occasionally gullible. It is, for example, most doubtful whether a painted wooden whistle really had belonged to Diane de Poitiers or a tobacco pouch to Sir Walter Raleigh, as Wallace believed, but such agreeably romantic fallacies were very few.

Tauzia's collection was better focussed. It contained a number of fifteenth- and sixteenth-century Italian paintings, a few Old Master drawings, and a collection of illuminated manuscript cuttings and Italian bronzes from the same period. Tauzia was far more of a scholar than Nieuwerkerke and his collection had been modestly housed, where Nieuwerkerke's was lavishly displayed. In the early 1860s he had travelled extensively in Italy acquiring Renaissance paintings not only for the Louvre but for himself, and the beautiful Foppa fresco from the Palazzo Mediceo in Milan, *The young Cicero reading*, might narrowly have missed entering the French national collection.

Wallace installed his antiquities in Hertford House in 1875, after the House had been extended to receive his vast collections. Recognising how remote they were from his father's sentimental and pleasurable taste, he isolated his new collection in what he called the Sixteenth Century Room (today the northern half of gallery 3) and arranged a dense display evoking a romantic concept of the past. Next door was his Smoking Room with its oriental Minton tiles (now gallery 4, the tiles, alas, removed in 1937), and it was not, presumably, accidental that these rooms should have been as far removed as possible from Lady Wallace's private suite, nor that they were excluded from the itinerary followed by the select visitors admitted to Hertford House. But this was to emphasize the distinct and private character of the rooms, rather than to suggest that their content was, in any way, an unworthy addition to his father's collection.

THE YOUNG CICERO READING
Vincenzo Foppa (active 1456, died
Brescia 1515/16)
Plaster, 99 × 133 cm; *c*1464

The only surviving fresco fragment
from the Palazzo Mediceo, Milan; it
was cut from the wall *c*1863.
From the Tauzia collection (P538;
gallery 3)

1

FRONTISPIECE FOR BOETHIUS, *DE CONSOLATIONE PHILOSOPHIAE*
The Master of Coëtivy (active in France, later 15th century)
Vellum, 24.1 × 16.5 cm; *c*1460-70
(M320; gallery 3)

2

INITIAL A WITH *GALEAZZO MARIA SFORZA IN PRAYER*
Cristoforo da Preda (active in Milan 1470, died before 1486)
Vellum, 22.5 × 19 cm; *c*1477
(M342; gallery 3)

Both these illuminations came from the Tauzia collection; they were cut from manuscripts probably in the late 18th century

3

ST ROCH
Carlo Crivelli (born Venice 1430/5, died Ascoli Piceno? 1495)
Panel, 40 × 12 cm; *c*1493

Probably part of a polyptych incorporating a number of saints. From the Tauzia collection (P527; gallery 3)

1

2

3

4

THE CRUCIFIXION
The Master of the Mège Diptych
(active in Paris 1325-50)
Ivory, 13.5 × 10.5 cm

A leaf from a diptych. From the
Nieuwerkerke collection (S249;
gallery 4)

5

ST PETER WITH PIERRE II DE BEAUJEU;
ST ANNE WITH ANNE OF FRANCE
6
THE EMPEROR CHARLEMAGNE;
ST LOUIS OF FRANCE
French
Translucent enamel on gold; each
panel 4.5 × 3.7 cm; *c*1500

Originally the shutters of a
devotional triptych; when closed
they showed Charlemagne and
Louis, and when open the donors,
Pierre de Beaujeu and his wife
Anne of France, with their patron
saints. The figures recur in an
altarpiece in Moulins Cathedral by
the Master of Moulins, a follower of
Hugo van der Goes. Bought by Sir
Richard Wallace in 1872 (XII A 68;
gallery 3)

7

CHALICE
French
Glass with enamelled, gilt and
mould-blown decoration, 22.5 cm
high; *c*1550

Probably made by Venetian
craftsmen working in France. From
the Nieuwerkerke collection (XXV B
96; gallery 3)

8

EWER
Venetian
Clear and opaque white glass with
gilt decoration, 27 cm high; late
16th century

From the Nieuwerkerke collection
(III E 174; gallery 3)

4

5

6

7

8

1
DISH
Deruta
Tin-glazed earthenware (maiolica),
39 cm diameter; *c*1500-25

The forlorn girl is accompanied by
a scroll inscribed (in translation)
'My heart has only hope'. From the
Nieuwerkerke collection (C27;
gallery 4)

2
DISH
Gubbio by Giorgio Andreoli
Tin-glazed earthenware (maiolica),
44.5 cm diameter; signed and dated
6 April 1525 on the reverse

The decoration is taken from three
engravings, one after Raphael.
Bought by Sir Richard Wallace in
1872 (C66; gallery 4)

1

2

3
WINE COOLER
Urbino, by Flaminio Fontana?
Tin-glazed earthenware (maiolica),
40 cm high, 71 cm wide; 1574

Signed F.F.F. on the foot. The inside
is decorated with a naval battle
derived from a fresco by Taddeo
Zuccaro showing the capture of
Tunis. Bought by Sir Richard
Wallace in 1875 (C107; gallery 4)

4
CHARLES IX OF FRANCE
Germain Pilon (born Paris 1537,
died Paris 1590)
Bronze, 62 cm high; *c*1574

Charles IX succeeded his elder
brother François II in 1560 and was
succeeded in 1574 by his younger
brother Henri III, the last of the
Valois kings of France. Bought by
the fourth Marquess of Hertford in
1865 (S154; gallery 3)

3

4

5

SEATED NYMPH

Giovanni Fonduli da Crema
(active in Padua 1468-84)
Bronze with gilt drapery, 20.5 cm
high

The signature OPUS IO CRE on the
back of the throne is unique. The
pose is taken from a classical
original, sometimes associated with
a *Dancing faun* who entices the
nymph as she adjusts her sandal.
Bought by the fourth Marquess
of Hertford before 1865 (S72;
gallery 4)

6

HERCULES

Francesco da Sant'Agata (active
in Padua 1491-1528)
Boxwood, 29 cm high; 1520

In 1560 this celebrated figure, then
in the collection of a Paduan
antiquary, was described as having
been carved in 1520. From the
Nieuwerkerke collection (S273;
gallery 4)

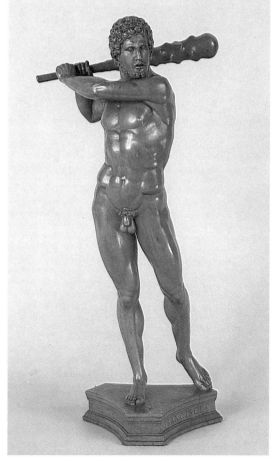

5

6

1

APOLLO AND THE MUSES
Martial Courtois (died *c*1592)
Limoges enamel, 56.5 × 42 cm

The design is copied from an
engraving of a design by Luca
Penni, itself deriving closely from
the painting by Raphael in the
Vatican (III F 268; gallery 3)

2

The underside of APOLLO AND THE
MUSES

3

LARGE OVAL DISH
**French; by a follower of Bernard
Palissy**
Lead-glazed earthenware,
14.5 × 19.5 cm; late 16th century
(C174; gallery 4)

4

MARGUERITE DE FRANCE AS MINERVA
Jean de Court (active 1555-85)
Limoges enamel, 20 × 15.5 cm;
1555

Signed and dated on the reverse.
Marguerite de France, daughter of
François I and patroness of poets,
is shown as the Goddess of Wisdom.
From the Nieuwerkerke collection
(III F 253; gallery 3)

1

2

3

22

4

5

6

7

5

CLAUDE DE LORRAINE, DUC DE GUISE, AND ANTOINETTE DE BOURBON, DUCHESSE DE GUISE

French

Wax, each panel 12 × 8 cm; *c*1540

The earliest known French wax portraits. The hinged leather case bears the sitters' monograms, CG and AB, on the reverse sides. Bought by Sir Richard Wallace in 1874 (S417; gallery 3)

6

CUP AND COVER

Augsburg; probably by David Altenstetter (1573–1617)

Silver and silver-gilt, with translucent enamel arabesques, 22.5 cm high; *c*1600 (XII A 112B; gallery 3)

7

PENDANT JEWEL

German

Translucent enamels on gold, encrusted in glass, 4.2 × 6.5 cm overall; early 17th century (XII A 93; gallery 4)

Arms and Armour

The magnificent collection of European arms and armour in the Wallace Collection is amongst the most valuable of its kind in the world, outside the great dynastic armouries of Vienna, Madrid, Paris and the Tower of London. It is supplemented by a select representation of Oriental arms and armour. The first was acquired almost entirely by Sir Richard Wallace, the second was gathered principally by his father, the fourth Marquess of Hertford.

Wallace's European armoury came largely from two sources, the collection of the comte de Nieuwerkerke (see MEDIEVAL AND RENAISSANCE), which he bought in 1871, and the collection formed by Sir Samuel Rush Meyrick (1783-1848) of Goodrich Court, Herefordshire. Meyrick had been a pioneer collector of arms and armour and had introduced the subject as a proper field of study. His collection had passed to his kinsman General Augustus Meyrick who sold it privately in 1871, the principal pieces being acquired by the Paris dealer Frédéric Spitzer, from whom Wallace purchased them in 1871. Although such sources ensured a considerable degree of quality, it seems likely that Wallace had no profound knowledge of European armour, and that his purchases reflected another aspect of his enthusiasm for the medieval and Renaissance periods which his father had so studiously neglected. His appreciation of armour was probably confined to an admiration of form and craftsmanship, for the two main strengths of his armoury are the number of finely decorated pieces of armour for parade, tournament and use in the field, and the series of finely wrought sixteenth- and seventeenth-century daggers and swords.

Although most of the armour dates from the fifteenth and sixteenth centuries, there is a fourteenth-century visored helmet (A69), whose aggressive shape is formed of unadorned steel. The greatest period of the armourer's craft is generally regarded as the later fifteenth century, when Italian and German craftsmen exploited subtle shapes with discreet decoration. The equestrian armour (A21) shows the pointed, cusped edges and shell-like fluting of the German Gothic style, while the crossbow (A1032) demonstrates another aspect of fine German craftsmanship in the relief carvings of religious and secular scenes on the tiller. The later German composite armour for man and horse (A29) is more ornate with etched and gilt decoration and black painted panels. From the mid-sixteenth century comes the magnificent etched and gilt helmet (A188), part of the 'Golden Garniture' made in Augsburg for the Hapsburg Emperor. Perhaps the richest decoration of all appeared in Milan in the sixteenth century when embossed, gilt and damascened pieces, like the half armour (A51), were made for ceremonial purposes. The only English school of armourers was founded by Henry VIII who brought to London a number of German and Italian craftsmen to form his new Royal workshops; the fine suit of Greenwich armour (A62) was made there in the late sixteenth century.

The arms in the collection display the same elaborate decoration and craftsmanship. The richly decorated ceremonial dagger presented to Henri IV by the city of Paris (A790) is one of very few pieces not from the Nieuwerkerke or Meyrick collections, having been bought by Sir Richard Wallace at a Paris auction in 1877, one of his last purchases. It seems to typify his taste; it is of the greatest historical interest and it is more a work of art than a weapon. The swords made for Cosimo de' Medici (A710) and Henry, Prince of Wales (A511), are similarly of the utmost historical interest. The stocks of two French flint-lock pistols (A1209-10), made for Louis XIV probably about 1660, are miraculously carved with scenes from the lives of Hercules and Samson, and one of the latest pieces in the collection, the Boutet double-barrelled flint-lock gun (A1127), which may have belonged to the Tsar Nicholas I, bears very fine silver-gilt mounts in the Empire taste.

The Oriental arms and armour were collected deliberately for their decoration and exotic associations. The Emperor Napoleon III and his half-brother the duc de Morny, besides the fourth Marquess of Hertford, were enthusiastic collectors of such pieces during the 1860s. The appeal of the exotic, also reflected in contemporary French painting and writing, was an aspect of Romanticism stimulated by particular historical events; Napoleon's Egyptian campaigns and the Greek War of Independence had aroused a general interest in the Ottoman Empire, and the French conquest of Algeria in 1830 had brought the Arab world into sharper focus. Many of the pieces acquired by Second Empire collectors were near contemporary, but amongst Lord Hertford's acquisitions were the two particularly fine daggers here illustrated, dating from the fifteenth and seventeenth centuries: the Mogul example (OA1409) with a hilt of pure gold set with rubies and precious stones, and the Persian (OA1414) with a blade encrusted and inlaid with gold. The study of such weapons is still in comparative infancy, though much more is now known than in Lord Hertford's time.

When Wallace installed the armouries in Hertford House in 1875 he displayed the pieces arranged in decorative panels on the walls or as free-standing sculpture (see illustration, p.14). This was another indication of the nineteenth-century attitude to arms and armour; an armoury evoked a romantic past, but was not a centre for academic study. Today's display, whilst inspired by Wallace's original scheme, also accommodates a more informed interest.

GOTHIC WAR HARNESS FOR MAN
AND HORSE
South German
Steel, chiselled and fluted; late 15th
century

Though restored in the 19th
century, this shows something of
the splendour and elegance of the
finest German Gothic armour.
From the Nieuwerkerke collection
(A21; gallery 6)

1

CROSSBOW
Bavarian

Steel bow, the tiller overlaid with horn carved in imitation of ivory, 72 cm long; *c*1450-70

This remarkable bow belonged at one time to the Völs Colonna family in the South Tyrol. From the Meyrick collection (A1032; gallery 7)

2

VISORED BASCINET
Milanese?

Steel embossed; *c*1390-1410

This head-piece was scientifically designed to deflect enemy weapons. From the Meyrick collection (A69; gallery 7)

3

HUNTING FALCHION
Italian

Steel, parcel gilt, with agate grip; mid 16th century

Listed in the Medici armoury in 1639. The blade is etched with the arms of Cosimo I as used between 1546 and 1569. From the Nieuwerkerke collection (A710; gallery 6)

1

2

3

4
CLOSE HELMET FOR TOURNAMENT
ON FOOT
Augsburg
Steel with etched and gilt
decoration; 1555

Probably made by Conrad Richter
of Augsburg for the Emperor
Ferdinand I. From the
Nieuwerkerke collection (A188;
gallery 6)

4

LIGHT FIELD ARMOUR WITH EXTRA
PIECES
**Greenwich Royal Workshops, by
Jacob Halder**
Steel, etched, russeted and gilt;
*c*1587

Halder was Master Workman of the
Almain Armoury at Greenwich
from 1576 until his death in 1608.
This armour was made possibly for
Thomas Sackville, Earl of Dorset.
From the Meyrick collection (A62;
gallery 6)

COMPOSITE ARMOUR FOR MAN AND
HORSE
South German
Steel, etched, gilt and painted
black; mid 16th century

A composite armour made up from
at least eight different armours
originally made for Otto Heinrich,
Count Palatine of the Rhine
(1502-59). It was taken from his
castle at Neuburg in Bavaria by the
French in 1800. From the Meyrick
collection (A29; gallery 5)

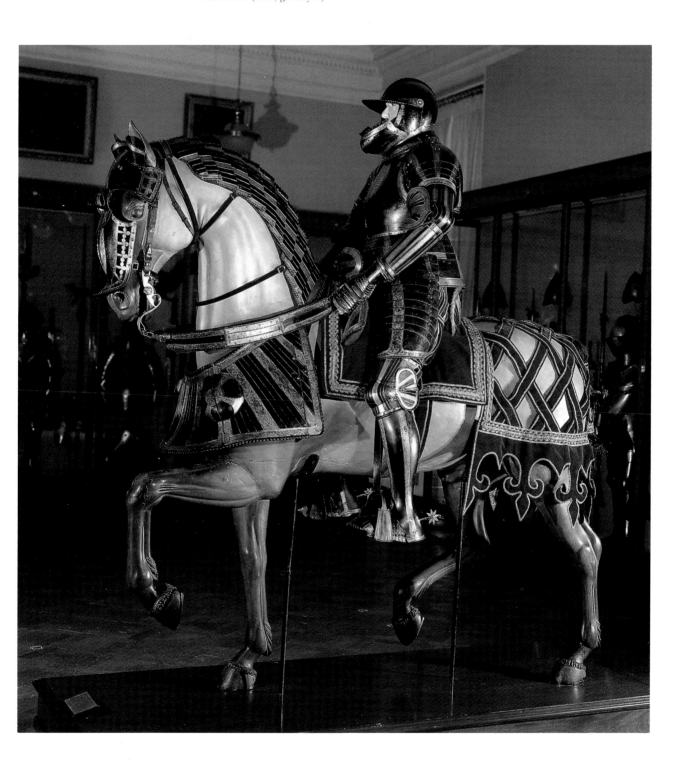

1

HALF ARMOUR
Milanese
Steel, etched and gilt; *c*1587

Made for Wolf Dietrich von
Raitenau who became Prince-
Bishop of Salzburg in 1587. Possibly
by Pompeo della Chiesa, one of the
most celebrated Milanese
armourers. From the Meyrick
collection (A60; gallery 6)

2

GORGET
Milanese
Steel, embossed, chased, blued, gilt,
and plated with silver; *c*1610

The decoration derives from
engravings of battle scenes by
Antonio Tempesta (A238; gallery 6)

3

DAGGER OF HENRI IV OF FRANCE
French
Steel, with mother-of-pearl inlay
and gold counterfeit damascening,
24 cm long; *c*1598-1600

Presented to Henri IV by the City
of Paris in 1600 on the occasion of
his marriage to Marie de Médicis;
their initials appear on the hilt.
Bought by Sir Richard Wallace in
1877 (A790; gallery 6)

1

2

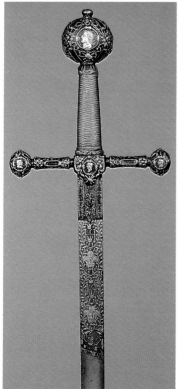

3

4

5

4

SWORD OF HENRY PRINCE OF WALES

English hilt; **German** blade **by Clemens Horn**

Steel, decorated with silver and gold, 82 cm long; *c*1610-12

The Prince of Wales's feathers on the blade indicate a date after 1610 when Henry became Prince of Wales; he died in 1612. The mark of Clemens Horn of Solingen appears twice on the blade (A511; gallery 6)

5

EMBOSSED HALF ARMOUR

Milanese; probably by Lucio Piccinino

Steel, embossed, gilt and damascened in gold and silver; *c*1570

This splendid armour would have been worn only for parade use on foot. From the Meyrick collection (A51; gallery 6)

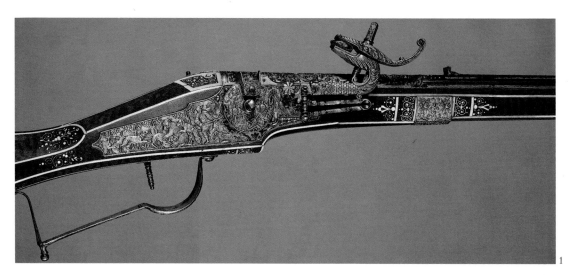

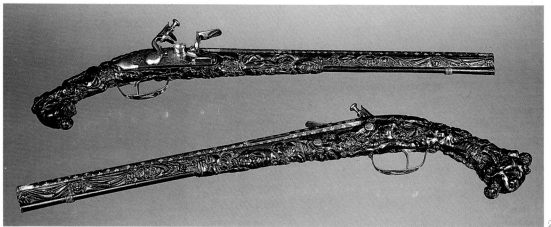

1

WHEEL-LOCK GUN
Munich; by Daniel Sadeler and Hieronymus Borstorffer
The lock finely chiselled and gilt; the butt of snakewood, inlaid with ivory; 170 cm long overall; *c*1620

From the Nieuwerkerke collection (A1090; gallery 5)

2

PAIR OF FLINT-LOCK PISTOLS
French
Stock of dark carved walnut; the breech engraved and damascened in gold; the barrel blued and powdered with gold fleurs-de-lys; 59.7 cm long overall; *c*1660

Made for Louis XIV, probably to celebrate the capture of Dunkirk in 1658 (A1209-10; gallery 5)

3

DOUBLE-BARRELLED FLINT-LOCK GUN
French; by Nicolas Noël Boutet
(1761-1833)
The breech damascened, the stock of carved walnut with silver-gilt mounts; 122.4 cm long overall; *c*1805

The barrel was made by one of the Leclerc family. Boutet was one of the leading Napoleonic gun-makers (A1127; gallery 5)

4

DAGGER
Indian, Mogul
Hilt of pure gold inset with table diamonds, rubies and emeralds; the finial set with rubies and emeralds, and cabochon rubies round the grip; above the blade of watered steel are jewelled animals' heads; 37.5 cm long; early 17th century

The richness of this dagger indicates that it was made for the Mogul Court (OA1409; gallery 8)

5

DAGGER
Iranian
Haft of white jade inlaid with gold, the blade of watered steel with gold filigree and encrusted gold decoration; 34.3 cm long; 1496-97

The silver band inset with greenstone below the hilt is a later addition. The earliest known dated weapon from Iran, the blade is inscribed with the Islamic date 902 (1496-97 in the Christian calendar) (OA1414; gallery 8)

4

5

Old Master Paintings

The greatest European Old Masters are represented in the Wallace Collection, and the long picture gallery in which they are principally displayed, running across Hertford House on the north side, is one of the finest individual rooms of paintings anywhere in the world. Hanging at eye level on the two long walls and at the east end are masterpieces by Rubens, Van Dyck, Velázquez, Murillo, Claude, Poussin, Philippe de Champaigne and Titian, while on the west wall hang a number of distinguished English eighteenth-century portraits by Gainsborough and Reynolds. Nearly all these pictures were acquired by the fourth Marquess of Hertford, but he had also inherited several fine pictures from previous generations of his family.

The first Marquess of Hertford had acquired six paintings by Canaletto in the artist's lifetime (see P499). This was a characteristic English eighteenth-century taste, led by George III who may, indeed, have inspired the Marquess, a loyal Tory courtier, to buy. The second Marquess bought the charming *Nelly O'Brien* by Reynolds, one of his most delicate and attractive portraits, and was given Gainsborough's gracious full-length of *Mrs Robinson* by George IV, as described in the introductory essay. But the most remarkable Old Master inherited by the fourth Marquess was the great *Perseus and Andromeda* by Titian, bought by his father at Christie's in 1815. It was by no means a typical purchase, for his father's taste was essentially for seventeenth-century Dutch cabinet pictures, and while today it may seem to have been a very wise choice, at the time it was neglected. By 1850 it had lost its attribution and the fourth Marquess, living in Paris, seems to have been unaware of its existence in London. In 1870 it was listed as a Domenichino and Sir Richard Wallace innocently hung it above his bath in Hertford House for nearly twenty years. Not until 1899 was it rediscovered, by the first Director of the Wallace Collection, Sir Claude Phillips.

The fourth Marquess of Hertford used to say repeatedly that he liked only 'pleasing' pictures; scenes of violence or depictions of old age were not for him. One of his favourite painters was Murillo who had, he said, 'a rich, mellow quality I so much admire', beautifully exemplified here by the little *Marriage of the Virgin* and the larger *Adoration of the Shepherds*. The Old Masters he bought belonged to a traditional canon of taste; he ignored the discoveries of the nineteenth century, such as El Greco and Vermeer, while the fearful view of humanity expressed by the 'primitive' painters of the early Renaissance ran quite counter to his epicurean philosophy. Lord Hertford was confident and knowledgeable as a buyer. He attended, or was represented, at all the greatest sales of the time, in London, Paris and The Hague where, at the King of Holland's sale in 1850, he received a standing ovation after outbidding the

national museums of Belgium and France, as well as the Tsar of Russia, for the two very fine whole-length portraits by Van Dyck, *Philippe Le Roy* and *Marie de Raet*. Such important sales mattered greatly to Lord Hertford, who paid attention to distinguished provenances. In the early nineteenth century an unprecedented quantity of fine works of art, from France, Germany, Spain and Italy, had come on to the market following the alarms and upheavals of the French Revolution and the Napoleonic Wars. There were then very few public institutions bidding for such works, with the result that, for the next fifty years and more, the art market in Europe was spectacular and presented rich collectors such as Lord Hertford with unprecedented opportunities.

In 1857 Lord Hertford lent forty-four of his paintings to the great *Art Treasures* exhibition in Manchester, and his choice of twenty-six Old Masters may be taken to indicate his own favourites. There were five Murillos, four Van Dycks, three Velázquez, three Reynolds, two Rubens and single works by Salvator Rosa, Del Sarto, Poussin, Dughet, Champaigne, Sassoferrato and Gainsborough. Of these Murillo and more particularly Velázquez were not then as familiar as they are today, for Spanish pictures had only reached European markets after wholesale looting during the Peninsular War. Velázquez's beautiful portrait, *The lady with a fan*, had been taken from Madrid in 1801 by Lucien Bonaparte, one of Napoleon's brothers, and Murillo's *Marriage of the Virgin* was taken by another of his brothers, Joseph, from the Palacio Real in Madrid. Similarly the work of Philippe de Champaigne, one of the finest of French seventeenth-century painters, remained unfamiliar to English collectors since most of his grandest pictures had been commissioned by the French Crown or for French churches. Lord Hertford eventually acquired four of his works, the particularly imposing *Annunciation* coming from the sale of Cardinal Fesch, Napoleon's predatory uncle, which had lasted for two months in Rome in 1845. Poussin's magnificent *Dance to the music of time* also came from the Fesch sale. The Cardinal had taken it from the Rospigliosi collection in Rome, where it had been since it was painted in the mid-seventeenth century. The elegiac subject, suggesting the precarious progress of fortune, need not have disturbed Lord Hertford, but it remains one of his most serious pictures.

The acquisition of Rubens's *Rainbow landscape*, perhaps the greatest of Lord Hertford's Old Master paintings, provides a rather melancholy tale. In the later eighteenth century it had been, with an equally splendid pendant landscape by Rubens, in the Balbi Palace in Genoa. Both were taken during the Napoleonic Wars by an English dealer who sold them separately. When the *Rainbow* was sold in London by Lord Orford in 1856 the National Gallery, who already owned the

pendant, obtained special funds to buy it, but nothing could then withstand Lord Hertford's bidding and he duly acquired the painting for just under 5,000 guineas. Today these two magnificent companion pieces are both in London, within a mile of each other, but not together. To complete the irony, Lord Hertford never saw the *Rainbow* after he had acquired it; it was delivered to Hertford House, but he stayed in Paris until his death. Such *insouciance* was part of his nature, but it also seems to indicate how important possession was for him, as opposed to display.

PERSEUS AND ANDROMEDA
Titian (born Pieve di Cadore *c*1485, died Venice 1576)
Canvas, 183 × 199 cm; 1554-56

One of the six great *poesie* painted by Titian for Philip II of Spain. Bought by the third Marquess of Hertford in 1815, this great picture went unrecognised in the 19th century and hung for twenty years above Sir Richard Wallace's bath (P11; gallery 19)

1

2

1 and 2
RAINBOW LANDSCAPE
Peter Paul Rubens (born Siegen
1577, died Antwerp 1640)
Panel, 136 × 236 cm; c1638

Painted at the end of his life when
Rubens was living in his country
residence at Het Steen. The
contrast between the two halves of
the composition, a sunlit prosperity
on the left and a gloomy wood on
the right, suggests an analogy with
the Last Judgment, the rainbow
representing the Ark of the
Covenant. The companion piece is
in the National Gallery, London.
Bought by the fourth Marquess of
Hertford in 1856 (P63; gallery 19)

3
THE HOLY FAMILY WITH STS
ELIZABETH AND JOHN THE BAPTIST
Peter Paul Rubens (born Siegen
1577, died Antwerp 1640)
Panel, 138 × 102 cm; c1614

Painted for the Oratory of the
Archduke Albert in the Ducal
Palace in Brussels (which was burnt
down in 1731). Bought by the
fourth Marquess of Hertford in
1846 (P81; gallery 19)

4
THE BIRTH OF HENRI IV OF FRANCE
Peter Paul Rubens (born Siegen
1577, died Antwerp 1640)
Panel, 21.5 × 10 cm; c1628-30
(P523; gallery 16)

5
THE MARRIAGE OF HENRI IV OF
FRANCE AND MARIE DE MEDICIS
Peter Paul Rubens (born Siegen
1577, died Antwerp 1640)
Panel, 23 × 12.5 cm; c1628-30
(P524; gallery 16)

These two sketches were made for a
cycle of twenty-one large paintings
commissioned by Marie de Médicis
to illustrate the life of her dead
husband, Henri IV of France. The
cycle was never completed. A third
sketch for the series is also in the
Wallace Collection. Both these
panels were bought by the fourth
Marquess of Hertford in 1859.

3

4

5

1

Anthony van Dyck (born Antwerp
1599, died London 1641)
Canvas, 213 × 115 cm; 1631

Painted in Antwerp on the occasion
of her marriage to Philippe Le Roy
in 1631 when she was sixteen (P79;
gallery 19)

2

Anthony van Dyck (born Antwerp
1599, died London 1641)
Canvas, 213 × 114 cm; 1630

One of Van Dyck's noblest portraits,
Philippe Le Roy was Counsellor to
the Archduke Ferdinand. The
companion portrait of his young
wife was painted the following
year. Both portraits were bought by
the fourth Marquess of Hertford at
the King of Holland's sale in The
Hague in 1850 (P94; gallery 19)

1

1

1
THE MARRIAGE OF THE VIRGIN
Philippe de Champaigne (born
Brussels 1602, died Paris 1674)
Panel, 71.5 × 143.5; *c*1644

Almost certainly painted for the
Oratory of Anne of Austria, widow
of Louis XIII, in the Palais Royal.
The Oratory was dismantled *c*1752.
Bought by the fourth Marquess of
Hertford in 1865 (P119; gallery 19)

2
THE ANNUNCIATION
Philippe de Champaigne (born
Brussels 1602, died Paris 1674)
Canvas, 334 × 214 cm; *c*1645

A masterpiece from Champaigne's
early maturity, this picture may
have been commissioned for the
hôtel de Chavigny where Mansart
had built a new chapel in 1642-43.
Bought by the fourth Marquess of
Hertford in 1845 (P134; gallery 19)

1

A DANCE TO THE MUSIC OF TIME
Nicolas Poussin (born Les Andelys 1594, died Rome 1665)
Canvas, 82.5 × 104 cm; c1638

Commissioned by Cardinal Giulio Rospigliosi who probably devised the subject; Poverty, Labour, Wealth and Pleasure dance an eternal round to the music of Time. Bought by the fourth Marquess of Hertford in 1845, the subject unusually grave for his taste (P108; gallery 19)

1

2

LANDSCAPE WITH APOLLO AND MERCURY
Claude Gellée (born Chamagne 1600, died Rome 1682)
Canvas, 74.5 × 110.5 cm; 1660

This picture passed from the Landgraves of Hesse-Cassel to the Empress Josephine, before being bought by the fourth Marquess of Hertford in 1846 (P114; gallery 19)

3

RIVER LANDSCAPE WITH APOLLO AND THE CUMAEAN SIBYL
Salvator Rosa (born Naples 1615, died Rome 1673)
Canvas, 174 × 259 cm; c1655

Originally in the collection of Cardinal Mazarin; bought by the fourth Marquess of Hertford in 1850 (P116; gallery 19)

2

3

1

1

THE ADORATION OF THE SHEPHERDS
Bartolomé Esteban Murillo (born
Seville 1617, died Seville 1682)
Canvas, 147 × 218 cm; c1668

One of seven Murillos given by a
Genoese merchant, Giovanni
Beilato, to the Capuchin convent in
Genoa; two of the others are also in
the Wallace Collection. Bought by
the fourth Marquess of Hertford in
1846 (P34; gallery 19)

2

THE MARRIAGE OF THE VIRGIN
Bartolomé Esteban Murillo (born
Seville 1617, died Seville 1682)
Panel, 76 × 56 cm; c1670

Listed in the Royal Palace of
Madrid in 1772, and bought by the
fourth Marquess of Hertford in
1848 (P14; gallery 2)

2

3

3

LADY WITH A FAN
Diego Velázquez (born Seville
1599, died Madrid 1660)
Canvas, 95 × 70 cm; c1640

A rare example of Velázquez's
portraiture outside the Court circle
of Philip IV. There is no proof of
her identity, but she is evidently a
lady of quality. Bought by the
fourth Marquess of Hertford in
1847 (P88; gallery 19)

1

1

THE FALLS OF TIVOLI
Gaspard Dughet (born Rome 1615,
died Rome 1675)
Canvas, 99 × 82 cm; c1661

Acquired by Lord Ashburnham in
the early 18th century, this
landscape combines Roman
topography with the picturesque in
a manner then particularly admired
by English collectors. Bought by the
fourth Marquess of Hertford in
1850 (P139; gallery 19)

2

MISS NELLY O'BRIEN
Joshua Reynolds (born Plympton
1723, died London 1792)
Canvas, 126 × 110 cm; 1762-64

This affectionate and accomplished
study of a famous courtesan was
bought by the second Marquess of
Hertford in 1810 (P38; gallery 19)

3

MISS JANE BOWLES
Joshua Reynolds (born Plympton
1723, died London 1792)
Canvas, 91 × 71 cm; 1775

Bought by the fourth Marquess of
Hertford from the sitter's family in
1850 (P36; gallery 23)

2

3

47

1

1

MRS MARY ROBINSON (PERDITA)
Thomas Gainsborough (born
Sudbury 1727, died London 1788)
Canvas, 234 × 153 cm; 1781

Mrs Robinson was the first mistress
of the Prince of Wales, who
commissioned this portrait and
later, in 1818, presented it to the
second Marquess of Hertford – who
was amongst her later admirers
(P42; gallery 19)

2

MISS ELIZABETH HAVERFIELD
Thomas Gainsborough (born
Sudbury 1727, died London 1788)
Canvas, 126 × 101 cm; *c*1782

Bought from the sitter's family by
the fourth Marquess of Hertford in
1859 (P44; gallery 19)

3

MRS MARY ROBINSON (PERDITA)
Joshua Reynolds (born Plympton
1723, died London 1792)
Canvas, 77 × 64 cm; 1783-84

After 1783 Mrs Robinson
contracted a fitful paralysis
following a miscarriage, and
Reynolds's portrait suggests the
more contemplative character
which then emerged, contrasting
with Gainsborough's earlier
portrayal. Bought by the fourth
Marquess of Hertford in 1859 (P45;
gallery 19)

2

3

1

1

VENICE: THE BACINO FROM THE
GIUDECCA
Antonio Canaletto (born Venice
1697, died Venice 1768)
Canvas, 130 × 191 cm; c1740

Perhaps the finest of the six
paintings by Canaletto which
belonged to the first Marquess of
Hertford; they were listed in his
London house in Grosvenor Street
in 1768 (P499; gallery 13)

2

VENICE: SAN GIORGIO MAGGIORE WITH
THE GIUDECCA AND THE ZITELLE
Francesco Guardi (born Venice
1712, died Venice 1793)
Canvas, 70 × 93 cm; c1775
(P491; gallery 13)

3

VENICE: THE DOGANA WITH THE
GIUDECCA
Francesco Guardi (born Venice
1712, died Venice 1793)
Canvas, 70 × 93 cm; c1775
(P494; gallery 13)

Two of a set of four views of Venice
by Guardi which the fourth
Marquess of Hertford bought in
Paris in 1865. They had previously
been in a Russian collection.

2

3

Dutch Painting

The seventeenth-century Dutch paintings form a distinct section of the Wallace Collection, remarkable for its quality and the quiet composure of its subjects. The careful narration of daily life – music lessons, letter-writing, lace-making, or christening feasts – and the affectionate descriptions of enticing yet natural landscape views contrasted with contemporary Italian or French painting, and conveyed a certain resolute pride in the character and prosperity of a country but recently liberated from Catholic Hapsburg rule. Such paintings came to be particularly favoured by eighteenth-century French collectors who admired their fine execution and displayed them in rich gilt frames in settings whose elegance was far removed from the Dutch Protestant ethos. French collectors admired, for example, the Wouwermans *Horse fair* for the freshness and delicacy of its colour, and ter Borch's *Lady reading a letter* for its fine execution and beautiful drawing. Both these pictures were bought by the fourth Marquess of Hertford in Paris in the mid-nineteenth century, but it was his father, the third Marquess of Hertford, who had started the distinguished collection of Dutch pictures.

In the early years of the nineteenth century the third Marquess had bought many Dutch pictures from sales in London and Paris. He seems particularly to have liked small, highly finished cabinet pictures, such as Netscher's *Lace-maker*, and he also appears to have paid particular regard to their condition and provenance. This was the mark of a serious collector, but he also indulged in a certain amount of dealing, putting twelve of his Dutch pictures up for sale in 1807, but buying six of them back. By 1809 he was advising the Prince of Wales, later George IV, on the acquisition of Dutch pictures and regularly bidding for him at auction. His connoisseurship was one of his few admirable characteristics. There are twenty of his Dutch pictures in the Wallace Collection now, and the Wijnants *Hilly landscape* may exemplify their quality and fine condition. The tavern scene by Brouwer, *A boor asleep*, shows the coarser subjects which sometimes appealed to him as a Regency rake, but which decidedly would not appeal to his son, the fourth Marquess of Hertford.

When the fourth Marquess bought a Steen, for example, he did not seek the run-down interior of an alchemist's laboratory (such as had appealed to his father), but a beautiful girl prettily dressed in blue and yellow being taught to play the virginals. Her teacher, admittedly, is a rather lecherous figure, but the whole composition has a charm which was to appeal directly to Fragonard in the eighteenth century. Such a charm runs through all the fourth Marquess's Dutch acquisitions. The ter Borch *Lady reading a letter* and de Hooch's *Woman peeling apples* recall his declaration that he liked only pleasing pictures; such peaceful interiors with their beautiful soft light present an enviable tranquillity. Of his landscapes the great Ruisdael *Landscape with a waterfall* is deeply moving with its fusion of grandeur and melancholy. It once belonged to baron Vivant-Denon, Napoleon's Minister of Fine Arts, who preferred it to all his other pictures, and at his sale in 1826 it was described lovingly in terms redolent of Lamartine.

Lord Hertford would often pay what were considered to be high prices for his pictures, though such criticism came, of course, from envious quarters. Perhaps the most famous instance of his alleged extravagance was his purchase of '*The Laughing Cavalier*' for a price more than six times the estimate. Hals's portrait is now of world renown, but it was then little known, as indeed was the painter. It had been bought for 1,500 francs in 1822 by the comte de Pourtalès-Gorgier, a famous collector of his day, and when his collection was eventually sold in Paris in 1865 the *Laughing Cavalier* was specially engraved and singled out as an outstanding Dutch portrait. Both Lord Hertford and baron James de Rothschild, his neighbour in the rue Laffitte, wanted the picture and their sale-room rivalry resulted in Hertford having to pay 51,000 francs. The price may initially have contributed to its reputation, but in time the image quite took hold of the public imagination. It is a splendid and spirited portrait, with a swagger which every spectator envies.

Rembrandts were purchased by both the third and fourth Marquesses. In 1870, on the death of the fourth Marquess, there were twelve in the Hertford inventory, of which three had been bought by the third Marquess, but now only one is accepted as by Rembrandt. Each of the others was acquired in good faith by a knowledgeable collector, but few painters were subject to such optimistic misinterpretation as Rembrandt. As our knowledge of him advances so our perception is sharpened, and it now seems clear that of the Hertford Rembrandts at least three are by Flinck, one by Backer and one by Willem Drost, all reputable pupils of the master. Two more from the master's studio are unattributed, and two are later imitations. The single Rembrandt in the Collection, *The artist's son, Titus*, bought by the fourth Marquess at the King of Holland's sale in 1850, is one of his finest portraits. Quite apart from the beautiful warm colouring, the poignant image of the pale youth still conveys that intimacy which prevailed between the ageing and unhappy painter and his loyal and promising son. Of the many masterpieces the fourth Marquess acquired, none was greater than this.

THE HARPSICHORD LESSON
Jan Steen (born Leyden 1625/6,
died Leyden 1679)
Panel, 36.5 × 48.5 cm; *c*1660

Bought by the fourth Marquess of
Hertford in 1859 (P154; gallery 17)

1

A WOMAN PEELING APPLES
Pieter de Hooch (born Rotterdam
1629, died Amsterdam 1684)
Canvas, 71 × 54 cm; *c*1663

Bought by the fourth Marquess of
Hertford in 1848 (P23; gallery 17)

2

A LADY READING A LETTER
Gerard ter Borch (born Zwolle
1617, died Deventer 1681)
Canvas, 45 × 33 cm; *c*1662

Bought by the fourth Marquess of
Hertford in 1848 (P236; gallery 17)

3

THE LETTER-WRITER SURPRISED
Gabriel Metsu (born Leyden 1629,
died Amsterdam 1667)
Panel, 45 × 39 cm; *c*1662

Bought by the fourth Marquess of
Hertford in 1867 (P240; gallery 17)

1

2

3

4

6

5

4

THE LACE-MAKER
Caspar Netscher (born Prague? 1635/6, died The Hague 1684)
Canvas, 34 × 28 cm; 1664

Bought by the third Marquess of Hertford in 1804 (P237; gallery 17)

5

THE GREENGROCER
Willem van Mieris (born Leyden 1662, died Leyden 1747)
Panel, 40 × 34 cm; 1731

Bought by the fourth Marquess of Hertford in 1860 (P220; gallery 17)

6

INTERIOR OF THE OUDE KERK, DELFT
Emmanuel de Witte (born Alkmaar c1615/8, died Amsterdam 1692)
Panel, 61 × 44 cm; 1651

The earliest known dated church interior by de Witte. Bought by Sir Richard Wallace in 1872 (P254; gallery 17)

1

1
THE ARTIST'S SON TITUS
Rembrandt (born Leyden 1606,
died Amsterdam 1669)
Canvas, 68.5 × 57 cm; *c*1657

Painted at the time of Rembrandt's
bankruptcy, when Titus and
Hendrickje Stoffels were
administering the sale of his
pictures. The portrait has been
slightly reduced on the right.
Bought by the fourth Marquess of
Hertford in 1850 at the King of
Holland's sale in The Hague (P29;
gallery 19)

56

2

2

LANDSCAPE WITH WATERFALL
Jacob van Ruisdael (born Haarlem
1628/9, died Amsterdam 1682)
Canvas, 101 × 142 cm; *c*1670

One of Ruisdael's grandest
landscapes, this was bought by the
fourth Marquess of Hertford in
1850 (P56; gallery 19)

3

SUNRISE IN A WOOD
Jacob van Ruisdael (born Haarlem
1628/9, died Amsterdam 1682)
Canvas, 90 × 77 cm; after 1670

Bought by Sir Richard Wallace
between 1872 and 1874 (P247;
gallery 16)

3

1

1

A WOODED LANDSCAPE
Meindert Hobbema (born
Amsterdam 1638, died Amsterdam
1709)
Canvas, 56.5 × 50 cm; c1660-65

Bought by the fourth Marquess of
Hertford in 1865 (P95; gallery 17)

2

A HILLY LANDSCAPE
Jan Wijnants (born Haarlem
1631/2, died Amsterdam 1684)
Canvas, 56.5 × 50 cm; c1660-5

Bought by the third Marquess of
Hertford before 1807 (P249;
gallery 16)

2

3

4

3
THE FERRY BOAT
Aelbert Cuyp (born Dordrecht 1620, died Dordrecht 1691)
Panel, 72 × 90 cm; *c*1652-55

Bought by the fourth Marquess of Hertford in 1860 (P54; gallery 18)

4
CALM: DUTCH SHIPS COMING TO ANCHOR
Willem II van de Velde (born Leyden 1633, died London 1707)
Canvas, 169 × 233 cm; *c*1665-70

One of the finest of van de Velde's Dutch period pictures, before he settled to London in 1672/3. Bought by the fourth Marquess of Hertford in 1846 (P137; gallery 19)

1

THE CHRISTENING FEAST
Jan Steen (born Leyden 1625/6,
died Leyden 1679)
Canvas, 89 × 109 cm; 1664

Bought by Sir Richard Wallace in
1872 (P111; gallery 17)

2

THE SLEEPING SPORTSMAN
Gabriel Metsu (born Leyden 1629,
died Amsterdam 1667)
Canvas, 40 × 35 cm; later 1650s

Bought by the fourth Marquess of
Hertford in 1845 (P251; gallery 17)

3

A BOOR ASLEEP
Adriaen Brouwer (born Oudenarde
1605/6, died Antwerp 1638)
Panel, 37 × 28 cm

Bought by the third Marquess of
Hertford in 1804 (P211; gallery 16)

1

2

3

4

THE LAUGHING CAVALIER
Frans Hals (born Antwerp 1582/3,
Haarlem 1666)
Canvas, 83 × 67 cm; 1624

Hals' most famous picture was
bought by the fourth Marquess of
Hertford in Paris in 1865 for a very
high price, though it had previously
been little regarded. The unknown
sitter was twenty-six years old
when his portrait was painted; he
displays a wonderfully rich
embroidered jerkin, but only his
eyes are smiling (P84; gallery 19)

4

1

A SOUTHERN HARBOUR SCENE
Claes Pietersz. Nicolaes Berchem
(born Haarlem 1620, died
Amsterdam 1683)
Canvas, 83 × 104 cm; late 1650s

Bought by the fourth Marquess of
Hertford in 1868 (P25; gallery 18)

1

2

THE HORSE FAIR
Philips Wouwermans (born
Haarlem 1619, died Haarlem 1668)
Panel, 64 × 88 cm; c1665

This picture enjoyed a particularly
high reputation in France in the
18th century. It was bought by the
fourth Marquess of Hertford in
1854 (P65; gallery 18)

3

THE AVENUE AT MEERDERVOORT
Aelbert Cuyp (born Dordrecht
1620, died Dordrecht 1691)
Panel, 70 × 99 cm; early 1650s

This view was probably
commissioned for one of the
Meerdervoort family who lived in
the Huis te Meerdervoort which is
seen on the left. Bought by the
fourth Marquess of Hertford in
1868 (P51; gallery 18)

2

3

1

DEAD HARE AND PARTRIDGES
Jan Weenix (born Amsterdam 1640, died Amsterdam 1719)
Canvas, 91 × 74 cm; *c*1690

One of the many still lives by Weenix bought by the fourth Marquess of Hertford who once called such pictures 'agreeable rubbish for the country'; this he acquired in 1867 (P182; gallery 19)

2

FRUIT AND FLOWERS
Jan van Huijsum (born Amsterdam 1682, died Amsterdam 1749)
Panel, 81 × 60 cm; *c*1720?

Possibly bought by Sir Richard Wallace in 1872 (P207; gallery 15)

3

PEACOCKS AND DUCKS
Melchior de Hondecoeter (born Utrecht 1636, died Amsterdam 1695)
Canvas, 211 × 177 cm; *c*1680?

Bought by the fourth Marquess of Hertford *c*1865 (P64; gallery 2)

1

2

3

French Eighteenth-Century Art

It is the outstanding collection of French fine and decorative art of the eighteenth century which particularly distinguishes the Wallace Collection. The refined elegance and ostentatious luxury of the *ancien régime* is vividly conveyed by the finest furniture, a wealth of Sèvres porcelain and gold boxes, and a collection of paintings by Watteau, Boucher, Fragonard and Greuze which is unmatched outside the Louvre. By far the greater part of this remarkable collection was acquired by the fourth Marquess of Hertford, whose circumstances and character allied him strangely with the *noblesse d'épée* under the later Bourbons. He was not burdened with responsibilities, his wealth was enormous, he owned apartments in the fashionable rue Laffitte in Paris, while his country residence, the château of Bagatelle in the Bois de Boulogne, had been built for the comte d'Artois, later Charles X of France, and he was the intimate friend of the Emperor Napoleon III. Added to which his sophistication, erudition and connoisseurship, the positive qualities which compensated for his misanthropy and selfishness, equipped him to re-enact the rôle of a Choiseul or a Conti. That times had changed, and that the French Revolution had intervened, was of little consequence to him. He had an almost naive love of beautiful things, an instinctive appreciation of the finest craftsmanship and a yearning for pleasurable works of art which, while making few demands on the intellect, appealed to a most exquisite sense of taste. Such criteria were entirely satisfied by the artists and craftsmen of the *ancien régime*.

It was ironic that the French Revolution of 1789 which overturned the *ancien régime* also created the opportunity for Lord Hertford to amass his collection of French art. The majority of the great French private collections of the eighteenth century were impounded between 1793 and 1795, when so many of their owners met their deaths at the guillotine, and despite a number of official sales, works of art were freely looted and privately sold. Fragonard's *Swing* and Greuze's *Votive offering*, for example, were seized in 1794 from the collections of the tax farmer Ménage de Pressigny and the comte d'Artois respectively. Many of these works of art came to be despised as emblems of the old order and there are tales of whitewashed Louis XV long-case clocks in butcher's shops and of students at the Ecole du Louvre, imbued with heroic republicanism and neo-classical theory, bombarding Watteau's disingenuous paintings. Not until the 1840s did the French begin to reappraise their eighteenth-century artists, and in the meantime great works of art had but precariously survived. Boucher's *Rising* and *Setting of the Sun*, two of Lord Hertford's finest pictures, had previously been bought from a bric-à-brac merchant in the 1820s for 380 francs (£15), and a set of four decorative panels by him, also in the Wallace Collection, made

into a folding screen. In 1847 Balzac published his novel *Le cousin Pons* in which a run-down violinist in a theatre orchestra gradually became the object of fierce interest to his richer friends and relations when they realised he had bought side tables by Riesener and drawings by Watteau for next to nothing in his youth.

Lord Hertford belonged to the next generation of collectors. He began buying seriously in the 1840s and by 1845 his pictures included Boucher's *Rape of Europa*, Greuze's *Broken mirror* and *Votive offering*, Fragonard's *Musical contest*, and a number of Lancrets. These were not, of course, the only things he was then acquiring – at a quite furious pace – but they are sufficient to indicate his remarkable penchant for the *ancien régime*. By 1850 he had his first three Watteaus, and in 1851 at the Pembroke sale in London he was buying furniture ranging from an early Boulle chest of drawers (F405) to a Sèvres-plaqued Louis XVI secretaire. It was already clear that he admired all of the French eighteenth century, from the solemn grandeur of Boulle to the delicate refinement of the Louis XVI period, from Watteau's insubstantial fantasies to Greuze's palpable sentimentality, and amid such broad sympathies it is not easy to identify more specific aspects of his French taste. His only criteria seem to have been those endemic to all discriminating collectors, a consistent regard for high quality, fine condition and a reputable provenance.

After the accession of Napoleon III in 1852 and the establishment of a traditional, if not reactionary, government, the French taste for the art of the *ancien régime* grew apace. Lord Hertford, as an old acquaintance of the Emperor, was freely received in the Court circles of the Second Empire, and he would have enjoyed seeing that the Empress Eugénie insisted on wearing Marie-Antoinette costume for her portrait by Winterhalter, and he may even have helped to persuade her to redisplay some of the fine eighteenth-century furniture from the Royal palaces. In 1860 and 1865 two remarkable exhibitions were held in Paris which effectively marked the reinstatement of French eighteenth-century art and an official confirmation of Lord Hertford's taste: a loan exhibition of paintings held by the dealer Martinet and another of applied art from the past organized by the *Union centrale des Beaux-Arts appliqués à l'Industrie* and called, attractively, *Le Musée Rétrospectif.* Lord Hertford was a conspicuous lender to both these exhibitions which provided the first opportunity for the French public to appreciate the extent of his collecting.

To Martinet in 1860 he lent ten paintings, including the two sets of Boucher pendants, the *Rising* and the *Setting of the Sun*, and the *Autumn* and the *Summer pastoral*. These are large and splendid pictures which show Boucher's confident fluency at its height, the first painted for Madame de Pompadour, the second

First floor

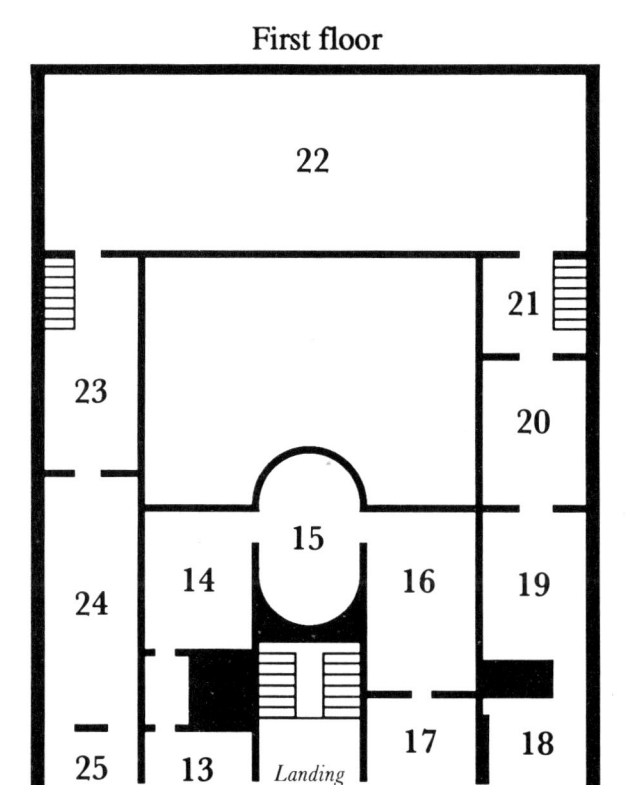

13-15	18th-century French paintings and furniture (English paintings in Gallery 13)
Corridor	Gold boxes, perpetual almanach and silver-gilt service
16	Sèvres porcelain and 18th-century French furniture
17	Canaletto and Guardi; 18th-century French furniture
18-21	Dutch and Flemish paintings
22	Titian, 17th-century paintings and English portraits
23	19th-century French paintings (also miniatures)
24 & 25	18th-century French paintings and furniture (miniatures in Gallery 24)

The Wallace Collection
Manchester Square, London, W1M 6BN
Tel.: 071-935 0687
Open: Mon.-Sat. 10a.m. - 5p.m.; Sun. 2p.m. - 5p.m.

Entrance is free, though donations towards the care of the Collection are very welcome. There is a free lecture programme; guided tours can be arranged for organized groups for a reasonable charge; and study days on aspects of the Collection are occasionally held.

THE WALLACE COLLECTION

The Wallace Collection is a national museum bequeathed to the nation in 1897 by Lady Wallace, widow of Sir Richard Wallace. It displays works of art acquired principally in the nineteenth century by the third and fourth Marquesses of Hertford and by Sir Richard Wallace (1818-90), son of the fourth Marquess. The Collection is displayed on the ground and first floors of Hertford House, the family's main London residence. An illustrated Guide is available in the shop.

Ground floor

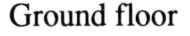

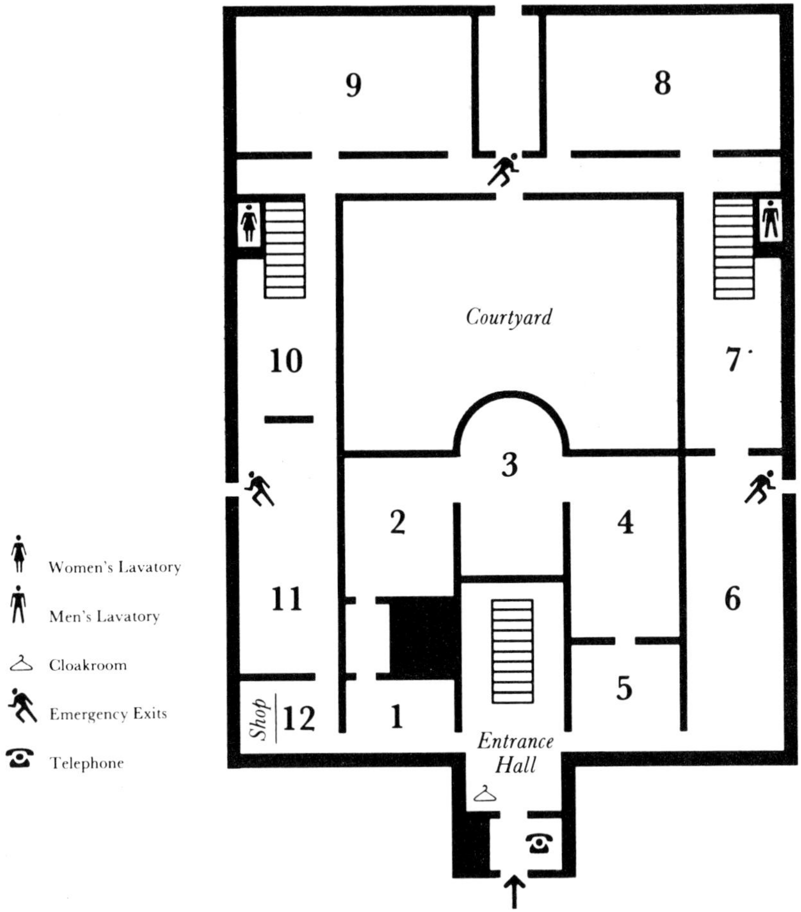

9
8
Courtyard
10
7
3
2
4
11
6
5
Shop
12
1
Entrance Hall
Women's Lavatory
Men's Lavatory
Cloakroom
Emergency Exits
Telephone

1 & Corridor	Bonington and early 19th-century paintings
2-4	French 18th-century furniture, paintings; Sèvres porcelain (Spanish and Dutch paintings in Gallery 4)
5	English paintings and 18th-century French furniture
6, 7 & Corridor	Medieval, Renaissance and Baroque works of art
8-11	Arms and armour (Orientalist paintings in Gallery 11)
12	SHOP & INFORMATION 19th-century English paintings

View in Gallery 12, showing A
GARNITURE OF THREE SEVRES VASES
AND TWO CANDELABRA IN FRONT OF A
WALL-MIRROR ABOVE THE
CHIMNEYPIECE

Two Sèvres vases of 1769 (C288-9)
flanking a *vase sirène* of *c*1776
(C333) with French candelabra of
*c*1785 (F134-5), on a Louis XVI
chimneypiece (F254) with a French
early 19th-century wall-mirror
(F439)

for the financier Trudaine, demanding and prestigious patrons. No other Englishman would then have dreamt of acquiring such paintings, and few French private collectors even then wished for such extravagant display. They remain the finest of Lord Hertford's many Bouchers and today they grace the imposing staircase and landing in Hertford House, wistful embodiments of pleasure and pretence. The Martinet exhibition also revealed to Lord Hertford other paintings in private hands, and within five years he had bought six of them, including the memorable Fragonards, *The souvenir* and *The swing*, which had belonged to the duc de Morny, Napoleon III's half-brother. They demonstrate all of Fragonard's wit, sophistication and assurance, and it is curious that Lord Hertford acquired four of his six Fragonards only in the last five years of his life.

His loan to the *Musée Rétrospectif* was quite massive, 288 numbered items, several of them composite. One hundred and forty items were Oriental arms and armour (see ARMS AND ARMOUR), but the rest were fine examples of applied art from the eighteenth century. The most imposing section numerically comprised 97 pieces of Sèvres porcelain, including many extravagant Rococo vases. His taste generally demanded such richly decorative pieces, rather than more functional services. He particularly looked for royal provenances, believing, for example, that the inkstand C488 had been used by Marie-Antoinette during her imprisonment in the Temple and paying an enormous price for a garniture of three vases (see C334) given by Louis XV to Prince Henry of Prussia. He had also acquired six pieces, two wine-coolers and four ice-cream coolers (C478), from the celebrated service commissioned by the Russian Empress Catherine II in 1776. Sèvres porcelain had been perhaps the least neglected aspect of French eighteenth-century taste and Lord Hertford had had to pay quite handsomely for all his pieces; nevertheless the following decades were to see a further and dramatic increase in its value, a circumstance Lord Hertford's loan helped to precipitate.

Lord Hertford also lent twenty-five pieces of furniture to the *Musée Rétrospectif*, and they included his greatest pieces, such as the Gaudreaus *commode* from Louis XV's bed-chamber at Versailles (F86), the contemporary *commode* with its extraordinary dragon mounts (F85), the wonderful Avignon clock by Boizot and Gouthière (F258) and, on a smaller scale, the perfume-burner of red jasper and gilt bronze by Gouthière which had once belonged to Marie-Antoinette (F292). Such pieces exemplified the highest achievements of the *ciseleurs* and *ébénistes* of the *ancien régime*, and their public exhibition must have aroused the respect and admiration of many visitors. Lord Hertford's particular passion for clocks was much in evidence, for he exhibited twenty-one, suggesting that there was some truth in the tale that he had over one hundred on a special platform in his bedroom in the rue Laffitte. At least the implication that he accumulated, rather than displayed or furnished, must have been correct. It is a curious fact that, although he was much concerned with the pedigree of his pieces, Lord Hertford did not then know that, for example, the *commode* by Gaudreaus (F86) had belonged to Louis XV, nor that another of his drop-front secretaires (F302) had belonged to Marie-Antoinette; it was only when the French Royal archives were attentively studied in the last fifty years that such distinctions were established.

Both the third Marquess of Hertford and Sir Richard Wallace contributed to the eighteenth-century French collection now in Hertford House. The third Marquess had been buying Boulle furniture and essentially functional pieces of Sèvres porcelain, such as the cup and saucer (C443), early in the nineteenth century, his taste being here influenced by that of the Prince of Wales (later George IV). Wallace bought a few good pictures, such as the two Fragonard children, *A boy as Pierrot* and *The young scholar*, and the charming miniature by Hall, *The painter's family*. Wallace, of course, was here following the example of his father, from whom he had learned so much and for whom, in his earlier years, he had acted virtually as sale-room agent and curator. In 1860 his uncle, Lord Henry Seymour, bequeathed to him the little Watteau, *Harlequin and Columbine*, which remains one of the most charming of this master's works in the Wallace Collection.

When the Wallace Collection was first opened to the public in 1900 it was the French art that attracted most comment. The art of the *ancien régime* was unfamiliar to English eyes, and the voluptuous pleasures described by Boucher and Fragonard were somewhat opposed to the values underwritten by Queen Victoria in the final year of her reign. 'The public has grown rich in Boucher', commented one critic, 'much beyond the desires of the judicious'. The opulence of the gold boxes, furniture and pictures is perhaps more congenial to today's less inhibited visitors.

MANTEL CLOCK
French
Gilt bronze, enamel and Carrara
marble; 60 cm high; *c*1774

Showing the young Louis XVI
being instructed by Minerva,
Goddess of Wisdom. Bought by the
fourth Marquess of Hertford before
1865 (F259; gallery 1)

1

1

MADAME DE VENTADOUR WITH
PORTRAITS OF LOUIS XIV AND HIS
HEIRS
French
Canvas, 128 × 161 cm; c1715-20

Madame de Ventadour protected
the infant Louis XV from the
epidemic which took the lives of
the Grand Dauphin, the duc de
Bourgogne and the duc de
Bretagne, Louis XIV's son,
grandson and eldest great-grandson.
The Grand Dauphin and
Bourgogne appear in this
commemorative portrait (P122;
gallery 11)

2
LOUIS XIV
Antoine Coysevox (born Lyons
1640, died Paris 1720)
Marble; 74 cm high; c1686

(S21; gallery 24)

3

3

CHARLES LE BRUN

Antoine Coysevox (born Lyons 1640, died Paris 1720)
Terracotta, 66 cm high; 1676

A full-sized model exhibited to the Académie Royale in 1676, from which Coysevox carved the marble bust now in the Louvre. Le Brun was one of the founders of the Académie and the King's First Painter; this terracotta is, therefore, a major document of *le grand siècle* (S60; gallery 11)

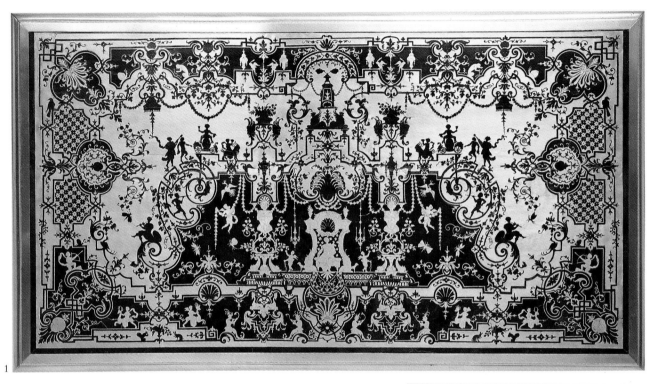

1

1

TOP OF A KNEE-HOLE WRITING TABLE

French

Veneered on oak with Boulle
marquetry of engraved brass and
tortoise-shell, 72.5 × 131.5 cm;
early 18th century

This elaborate design, showing
Apollo, lower centre, surrounded by
grotesques and animals, is taken
from an engraving after Jean
Berain (F57; gallery 16)

2

DECORATIVE PANEL FROM A
WARDROBE

André-Charles Boulle (born 1642,
died Paris 1732)

Veneered on oak with Boulle
marquetry of engraved brass and
tortoise-shell; c1695-1700

One of the panels on the two doors,
showing Apollo and Daphne (F61;
gallery 3)

3

CHEST OF DRAWERS

French

Veneered on oak with Boulle
marquetry of engraved brass on
tortoise-shell over red pigment;
88 cm high, 130 cm wide; c1700

The design, which imitates an
antique sarcophagus, was in fact
taken from an engraving after Jean
Berain (F405; gallery 19)

4

TOILET MIRROR BACK

André-Charles Boulle (born 1642,
died Paris 1732)

Oak veneered with ebony, engraved
brass and tortoise-shell,
75.5 × 55 cm; 1713

This fine mirror was delivered to
the duchesse de Berri in 1713; it
later belonged to the wife, and then
to the daughter, of the celebrated
diarist the duc de Saint-Simon.
Bought by the fourth Marquess of
Hertford in 1868 (F50; gallery 11)

2

3

4

5

5

INK-STAND
French
Veneered on oak with Boulle
marquetry of engraved brass and
tortoise-shell, with chased and gilt
bronze mounts, 39 × 60 cm; 1710

Made in 1710 for the Guild of
Barber-Surgeons in Paris, the
names of whose officers are
inscribed round the four sides
(F49; gallery 24)

73

TIME SAVING TRUTH FROM FALSEHOOD
AND ENVY
François Lemoyne (born Paris
1688, died Paris 1737)
Canvas, 149 × 114 cm, enlarged to
181 × 148 cm; 1737

Lemoyne's last picture, on which he
had been working within hours of
taking his own life. It was enlarged
*c*1760 to make up a set of four
Lemoynes then owned by the
financier Bouret. Bought by the
fourth Marquess of Hertford in
1851 (P392; gallery 11)

André-Charles Boulle (born 1642, died Paris 1732)
Veneered on oak with ebony and marquetry of brass and tortoise-shell; with bronze mounts chased and gilt; 302 cm high; c1715

This grand wardrobe and its companion were listed in Boulle's workshop in October 1715 (F429; gallery 2)

1

GILLES AND HIS FAMILY
Antoine Watteau (born
Valenciennes 1684, died Paris 1721)
Panel, 28 × 21 cm; c1716

A drawing for the central figure of
Mezzetin identifies the model as
Watteau's friend and patron Pierre
Sirois, but the composition is
fanciful rather than a family
portrait. Bought by the fourth
Marquess of Hertford in 1846
(P381; gallery 21)

2

HARLEQUIN AND COLUMBINE
Antoine Watteau (born
Valenciennes 1684, died Paris 1721)
Panel, 36 × 26 cm; c1716-18

The subject is a stock episode from
the *commedia dell'arte* where the
lively Harlequin makes advances to
Columbine. Bequeathed to Sir
Richard Wallace in 1860 by his
uncle, Lord Henry Seymour (P387;
gallery 21)

3

LES CHAMPS ELISEES
Antoine Watteau (born
Valenciennes 1684, died Paris 1721)
Panel, 31 × 42 cm; c1717-18

A much larger version of this
composition is also in the Wallace
Collection. Despite the title it is a
fanciful scene. Bought by the fourth
Marquess of Hertford in 1848
(P389; gallery 21)

4

LES CHARMES DE LA VIE (THE MUSIC
PARTY)
Antoine Watteau (born
Valenciennes 1684, died Paris 1721)
Canvas, 67 × 93 cm; c1718

The most satisfactory version of a
composition on which Watteau
worked for several years, expressing
delicate human relationships
through an analogy with music.
Bought by the fourth Marquess of
Hertford before 1854 (P410;
gallery 21)

1

2

3

4

77

1

1
MADEMOISELLE DE CAMARGO
DANCING
Nicolas Lancret (born Paris 1690,
died Paris 1743)
Canvas, 42 × 55 cm; 1730

One of the most celebrated dancers
of her day, she was twenty when
Lancret painted this portrait of her
in character; it was immediately
engraved. Bought by Sir Richard
Wallace in 1872 (P393; gallery 21)

2
CLOCK FACE
André-Charles Boulle (born 1642,
died Paris 1732)
Dial of gilt bronze with white
enamel plaques; 43 cm diameter;
1715

This model of clock (*pendule à
Vénus*) was listed in Boulle's
workshop in 1715. Bought by the
fourth Marquess of Hertford in
1870 (F93; gallery 2)

2

3

FETE IN A WOOD
Nicolas Lancret (born Paris 1690,
died Paris 1743)
Canvas, 64 × 91 cm; *c*1720-25

The composition reflects Lancret's
dependence on Watteau, under
whom he had briefly studied *c*1717.
Bought by the fourth Marquess of
Hertford in 1867 (P448; gallery 21)

4

PEDESTAL CLOCK
Probably by **André-Charles Boulle**
(born 1642, died Paris 1732)
Oak veneered with engraved brass
and tortoise-shell; gilt-bronze
mounts; 125 cm high; *c*1720-25

The flanking figures represent the
four continents, Europe, Asia,
Africa and America; above the clock
Cupid aims his arrows at whosoever
comes to tell the time. One of five
examples of this elaborate model.
Bought by the fourth Marquess
of Hertford in 1866-67 (F42;
gallery 24)

4

1

2

1
DEAD WOLF
Jean-Baptiste Oudry (born Paris
1686, died Beauvais 1755)
Canvas, 193 × 260 cm; 1721
(P626; gallery 12)

2
DEAD ROE
Jean-Baptiste Oudry (born Paris
1686, died Beauvais 1755)
Canvas, 193 × 260 cm; 1721
(P630; gallery 12)

Two of Oudry's finest compositions,
these pictures were bought by the
fourth Marquess of Hertford after
1860.

3
THE RAPE OF EUROPA
François Boucher (born Paris
1703, died Paris 1770)
Canvas, 231 × 274 cm; *c*1732-34

Painted for the *avocat* François
Derbais who owned at least eight
large Bouchers by 1735. Bought by
the fourth Marquess of Hertford in
1843 (P484; staircase)

4
BALUSTRADE
French
Forged iron and bronze, partly gilt,
93 cm high; *c*1740

Made for the grand staircase in the
Palais Mazarin (now the
Bibliothèque Nationale) when it
was acquired by Louis XV and
became the Bibliothèque du Roi. It
was probably designed by Robert de
Cotte. Removed between 1855 and
1862, it was acquired by the fourth
Marquess of Hertford and adapted
to the staircase of Hertford House
in 1872-75 (F68; staircase)

3

4

81

1

CHEST OF DRAWERS
Probably by **Antoine-Robert Gaudreaus** (born Paris *c*1682, died Paris 1746)
Veneered on oak with kingwood; gilt-bronze mounts, the top of breccia marble; 93 cm high; *c*1735-40

With a double bowed and *bombé* front and remarkable dragon mounts flanking the *espagnolette* head. Acquired by the fourth Marquess of Hertford before 1865 (F85; gallery 21)

2
CHEST OF DRAWERS, detail

1

2

CHEST OF DRAWERS
Antoine-Robert Gaudreaus (born
Paris *c*1682, died Paris 1746); the
mounts by **Jacques Caffiéri** (born
Paris 1678, died Paris 1755)
Veneered on oak with kingwood
and satiné; gilt-bronze mounts, the
top of serpentine marble; 89 cm
high; 1739

Made for Louis XV's new
bedchamber at Versailles in 1739,
the magnificent design closely
follows a drawing by one of the
Slodtz brothers, three of whom
were sculptors and designers for the
French court. Acquired by the
fourth Marquess of Hertford before
1865 (F86; gallery 21)

4
CHEST OF DRAWERS, detail

3

4

François Boucher (born Paris
1703, died Paris 1770)
Canvas, 260 × 199 cm; 1749
(P482; landing)

A SUMMER PASTORAL
François Boucher (born Paris
1703, died Paris 1770)
Canvas, 259 × 197 cm; 1749
(P489; landing)

These great pastorals, offering a
characteristic Boucher blend of
elegance and rusticity, were
commissioned by the financier
Trudaine for his new château at

Montigny-Lencoup, together with
four overdoors by Oudry which are
also in the Wallace Collection.
Bought by the fourth Marquess of
Hertford in 1852.

1

SHEPHERD AND SHEPHERDESS
REPOSING
François Boucher (born Paris
1703, died Paris 1770)
Canvas, 77 × 64 cm; 1761

Bought by the fourth Marquess of
Hertford in 1860 (P431; gallery 23)

2

VASE (*vase à tête d'éléphant*)
Sèvres
Porcelain, 38 cm high; 1756

Madame de Pompadour, an early
and loyal patron of the Sèvres
factory, had a pair of similar vases
in her extensive collection. The
extraordinary design conveys that
elegant extravagance and fine
craftsmanship which characterized
her taste (C246; gallery 14)

3

VASE, detail

1

2

3

4

4

MADAME DE POMPADOUR
François Boucher (born Paris
1703, died Paris 1770)
Canvas, 91 × 68 cm; 1759

Jeanne-Antoinette Poisson
(1721-64) became marquise de
Pompadour and *maîtresse en titre*
to Louis XV in 1745. Her lavish
patronage of the arts, in particular

of the Sèvres porcelain factory and
of Boucher, sustained the French
Rococo style. Behind her in this
portrait stands the sculpture of *Love
and Friendship* which she had
commissioned from Pigalle to
symbolize her later, platonic
relationship with the King. Bought
by the fourth Marquess of Hertford
in 1869 (P418; gallery 22)

THE SETTING OF THE SUN
François Boucher (born Paris 1703, died Paris 1770)
Canvas, 318 × 261 cm; 1752
(P486; staircase)

These extravagant and wonderful pictures show Apollo as God of the Sun leaving Tethys with her Nereids and Tritons in the river Ocean as he drives up the morning sun in his chariot drawn by four white horses, and then returning to her at nightfall. Boucher counted these amongst his most successful pictures. They were bought by the fourth Marquess of Hertford in 1855.

1
PERFUME-BURNER AND EGG-STEAMER
Sèvres
Porcelain, 23 cm high; 1758

Wine spirit could be heated in the
dish, allowing vaporised perfume
held in a cylinder above to perfume
and coddle an egg (C466; gallery
14)

2
BASKET
Vincennes
Porcelain, 29 cm high; 1753

Probably intended to hold porcelain
flowers or sugar fruits on a dining-
room table. Bought by the fourth
Marquess of Hertford in 1865
(C472; gallery 12)

1

2

3

4

6

5

3
INK-STAND
Sèvres
Porcelain, 38 cm wide; 1758

The terrestrial globe contained an inkwell, the celestial globe sand for drying the ink, the crown a bell, and its cushion a sponge for wiping nibs. Given by Louis XV to his daughter Marie-Adélaïde, it was bought by the fourth Marquess of Hertford in 1843 (C488; gallery 14)

4
FLOWER POT (*vase à dauphin*)
Sèvres
Porcelain, 21.5 cm high; 1756

The dolphins at the sides were introduced by the factory in 1754 to commemorate the birth of the Dauphin's second son, the future Louis XVI (C215; gallery 2)

5
VASE AND COVER (*vase Boileau*)
Sèvres
Porcelain, 49 cm high; 1758

Part of a garniture in the Wallace Collection, originally bought by Louis XV from the Sèvres factory in 1759 (C251; gallery 12)

6
FLOWER VASE (*cuvette à masques*)
Sèvres
Porcelain, 23 cm high; 1757

Intended to hold porcelain flowers (C225; gallery 14)

1

THE COMTESSE DE TILLIERES
Jean-Marc Nattier (born Paris
1685, died Paris 1766)
Canvas, 80 × 63 cm; 1750

Her silk pelisse is trimmed with
squirrel fur. Bought by the fourth
Marquess of Hertford (P453;
gallery 25)

2

CHEST OF DRAWERS, detail
René Dubois (born Paris 1737, died
Paris 1799)
Japanese lacquer and gilt bronze on
oak, width of detail 41 cm;
*c*1765-70

This oval forms the centre of the
drawer front and presents a slightly
eccentric combination of Japanese
lacquer and French neo-classicism.
Bought by Sir Richard Wallace in
1872 (F245; gallery 22)

1

2

3

3

Jean-Honoré Fragonard (born
Grasse 1732, died Paris 1806)
Canvas, 62 × 74 cm; *c*1754

Additions made to this canvas,
probably in the late 18th century,
were turned over in 1987 to reveal
this engaging composition by the
young Fragonard working in
Boucher's idiom. Bought by the
fourth Marquess of Hertford in
1842 as a Boucher (P471; gallery
21)

1

MADEMOISELLE DE CLERMONT *EN SULTANE*

Jean-Marc Nattier (born Paris 1685; died Paris 1766)
Canvas, 109 × 105 cm; 1733

A vivid example of French *turquerie* fashion; an elegant lady of the court, still wearing her ermine cloak, is painted as a sultana at the bath, surrounded by her slaves. Bought by the fourth Marquess of Hertford in 1858 (P456; gallery 12)

2

GOLD BOX
Paris
Lacquer and gold, 5.5 cm wide; *c*1779-80

The box bears the stamp of the goldsmith A-J Vachette. The decoration of Oriental lacquer shows the persistence of Oriental taste in the later 18th century (G60; first floor corridor)

3

GOLD BOX
Paris
Enamel with gold, 5 cm wide; 1749-50

The decoration is taken from a chinoiserie design by Boucher. The box bears the stamp of the goldsmith H Cheval (G8; first floor corridor)

4

THE GRAND TURK GIVING A CONCERT TO HIS MISTRESS

Carl Andrea van Loo (born Nice 1705, died Paris 1765)
Canvas, 73 × 91 cm; 1737

The harpsichordist is identified as the artist's wife, Christina Somnis, a singer of high reputation in her day; the musical score is that of Handel's new oratorio *Admeto*. Bought by the fourth Marquess of Hertford in 1867 (P451; gallery 12)

5

GOLD BOX
Paris
Painted enamel and gold; 5 cm wide; 1757-58

The box bears the stamp of the goldsmith Noël Hardivillers. The enamels are copied from a set of paintings by Carl van Loo made for Madame de Pompadour as overdoors for her château at Bellevue; they were shown at the Salon in 1753 and engraved in 1756 (G24; first floor corridor)

4

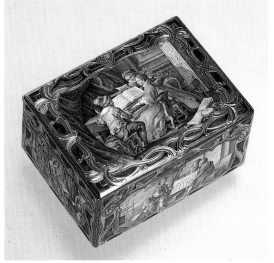

5

1

MANTEL CLOCK
Louis-Simon Boizot (born 1743, died Paris 1809) and **Pierre Gouthière** (born Bar-sur-Aube 1732, died Paris 1813)
Gilt bronze and marble, 68 cm high; 1771

Designed by Boizot and executed by Pierre Gouthière, this fine clock was presented by the city of Avignon to the marquis de Rochechouart on 29 December 1771. In 1768 he had received back the papal city of Avignon from Pope Clement XIII on behalf of Louis XV and had become its

governor. The figure representing the city of Avignon holds a wreath over the Rochechouart coat of arms, while the reclining male figure below represents the river Rhône and the seated female figure its tributary, the Durance. Bought by the fourth Marquess of Hertford before 1865 (F258; gallery 22)

2

4

2

MANTEL CLOCK

French

Sèvres porcelain with gilt bronze mounts on Carrara marble, 36 cm high; 1786

The Sèvres vase bears the date letter for 1786; the gilders' marks for Chauvaux *père* and *fils* appear on the cippus. Acquired by the fourth Marquess of Hertford before 1865 (F262 and C487; gallery 12)

3

MANTEL CLOCK

Augustin Pajou (born 1730, died Paris 1809) and **Etienne Martincourt** (active from 1762)

Gilt and patinated bronze, on Egyptian porphyry, 64 cm high

Designed by Pajou and executed by Martincourt. The figures show Love triumphing over the flight of Time. The hour is indicated by an arrow held by a cupid seated on the base. Bought by the fourth Marquess of Hertford in 1860 (F264; gallery 21)

4

MANTEL CLOCK

French

Gilt bronze, with medallions painted *en camaïeu*, 58 cm high; *c*1785

The clock movement is by Robert Robin, clockmaker to Louis XVI and Marie-Antoinette, who owned a similar clock. Bought by the fourth Marquess of Hertford in 1870 (F263; gallery 21)

97

1

A YOUNG SCHOLAR
Jean-Honoré Fragonard (born
Grasse 1732, died Paris 1806)
Canvas, 45 × 38 cm; c1775-8

One of several sentimental heads by
Fragonard, comparable to some
extent with those by Greuze,
though more plausible and
individual. Bought by Sir Richard
Wallace in 1872 (P455; gallery 21)

2

THE SOUVENIR
Jean-Honoré Fragonard (born
Grasse 1732, died Paris 1806)
Panel, 25 × 19 cm; c1775-8

The girl carves in the tree the
initials of her lover, whose letter
lies on the ground. Bought by the
fourth Marquess of Hertford in
1865 (P382; gallery 21)

3

THE SWING
Jean-Honoré Fragonard (born
Grasse 1732, died Paris 1806)
Canvas, 81 × 64 cm; 1767

This memorable picture was
devised and commissioned by an
unknown French nobleman (he was
not the baron de Saint-Julien, as
has been assumed in the past) who
wished to have the considerable
charms of his mistress celebrated on
canvas. Fragonard was
recommended to him as the best
painter for such a *louche* subject.
Bought by the fourth Marquess of
Hertford in 1865 (P430; gallery 21)

1

2

3

1

1

ROLL-TOP DESK

Jean-Henri Riesener (born Paris 1734, died Paris 1806)
Oak veneered with holly, sycamore, burr walnut, tulipwood and purplewood; gilt-bronze mounts; 140 cm high; 1769

This very fine desk was made for the young and vainglorious comte d'Orsay who had just acquired the hôtel de Clermont in the rue de Varenne. It closely imitates the celebrated *bureau du Roi* which Riesener, following the design of J-F Oeben, had then just completed for Louis XV at Versailles (where it remains). Like the King's desk, d'Orsay's is signed by Riesener in the marquetry (F102; gallery 25)

2

ROLL-TOP DESK, detail
The left-hand marquetry panel on the back of the desk

2

3

3

THE CHARIOT OF APOLLO
Philippe Caffiéri (born Paris 1714, died Paris 1774)
Gilt bronze, 45 cm high; c1767

This elaborate bronze appropriately surmounts a long-case clock by Nicolas Petit and J-J Lepaute; Apollo's chariot pulls the sun across the sky marking the passage of the day. The design recalls the celebrated gilt-lead figure of 1671 by Tuby in the Bassin of Apollo at Versailles (F270; gallery 23)

1
Claude-Joseph Vernet (born
Avignon 1714, died Paris 1789)
Canvas, 87 × 137 cm; 1754

Vernet's considerable contemporary
reputation was largely founded on
such agreeably terrifying images as
this, which were also particularly
prized by English collectors. Bought
by the fourth Marquess of Hertford
in 1869 (P135; gallery 14)

2
CARTONNIER, detail
René Dubois (born Paris 1737, died
Paris 1799)
Oak lacquered with *vernis Martin*,
partly gilt, with gilt-bronze mounts;
72 cm wide; *c*1765-70

The mount shows Cupid embracing
Psyche and the seated figures of
Peace and War. This cartonnier is
en suite with a writing table and
ink-stand also in the Wallace
Collection. Bought by the fourth
Marquess of Hertford in 1866
(F178; gallery 23)

3
LE PETIT PARC
Jean-Honoré Fragonard (born
Grasse 1732, died Paris 1806)
Canvas, 37 × 45 cm; *c*1764-5

This charming parkscape is
composed from drawings made in
the gardens of the Villa d'Este in
Tivoli in 1760. Bought by the
fourth Marquess of Hertford in
1867 (P379; gallery 21)

4
MUSICAL CLOCK
French
Gilt bronze, 91 cm high; *c*1760

The mount with a spaniel seizing a
hawk beneath a tree is particularly
fine. The banner of the French
Royal house above the base may
indicate that this clock was made
for a royal patron. It has a carillon
of fourteen bells which can play
thirteen different tunes. Bought by
the fourth Marquess of Hertford by
1865 (F97; gallery 24)

3

4

1

A BACCHANTE
J-B-J Augustin (born Saint-Dié
1759, died Paris 1832)
Ivory, 8 cm diameter; 1799

Copied from a painting by Greuze
of *c*1794 which probably belonged
to Augustin (M14; gallery 21)

1

2

3

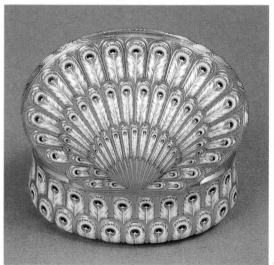

4

2

THE BROKEN MIRROR
Jean-Baptiste Greuze (born
Tournus 1725, died Paris 1805)
Canvas, 56 × 46 cm; 1763

This Hogarthian morality shows
the consequences of thought-
lessness; everything is in disorder,
and both the mirror and the girl's
reputation are shattered. Bought by
the fourth Marquess of Hertford in
1845 (P442; gallery 23)

3

GOLD BOX
Paris
Painted enamel and gold, 5.5 cm
wide; 1766-67

The box is stamped by the
goldsmith L Roucel. The enamels
are all after paintings by Greuze,
with his *Village bride* on the lid
(G44; first floor corridor)

4

GOLD BOX
Paris
Painted enamel and gold, 6 cm
wide; 1743-44

The box is stamped by the
goldsmith J Ducrollay. As the user
opened the box he presented the
opened peacock's tail to the
spectator (G4; first floor corridor)

5

GOLD BOX
Dresden
Cornelian mounted in gold with cameo relief and a secret slide with two miniatures; 6 cm wide; c1775

The miniatures, showing Voltaire and Madame du Châtelet, were rediscovered in 1976. The box, probably by J C Neuber of Dresden, was once in the collection of the

Empress Josephine. It was bought by Sir Richard Wallace in 1872 (G80; first floor corridor)

6

GOLD BOX
Paris
Gold, engraved and set with diamonds, 6 cm wide; 1752-54

Stamped by the goldsmith J Moynat (G16; first floor corridor)

7

GOLD BOX
Paris
Four colour gold, chased and engraved, 6 cm wide; 1757-58

This sumptuous box is stamped by the goldsmith J Frémin (G25; first floor corridor)

5

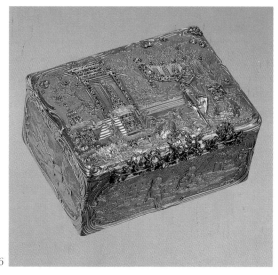

6

7

8

8

GOLD BOX
Paris
Gold with gouache miniatures on vellum, 7.5 cm wide; 1781-83

The miniatures, showing views of the château de Romainville, are by van Blarenberghe, either Louis-Nicolas or his son, Henri-Joseph. Bought by the fourth Marquess of Hertford in 1863 (G62; first floor corridor)

VOTIVE OFFERING TO CUPID
Jean-Baptiste Greuze (born Tournus 1725, died Paris 1805) Canvas, 146 × 113 cm; 1767

The girl's costume, her act of sacrifice, and the architectural details evoke antiquity, though such academism is not easily accommodated by Greuze's easy sentimentality. Bought by the fourth Marquess of Hertford in 1845 (P441; gallery 25)

1
VASE
Claude Michel Clodion (born
Nancy 1738, died Paris 1814)
Marble, 74 cm high

The orthodox classical shape is
relieved by the fleshy young
Bacchanals; as in Greuze's *Votive
offering* antiquity blends with the
ancien régime. Clodion produced
many versions of this basic design
between *c*1763 and 1785 (S32;
gallery 25)

2

2
PERFUME-BURNER
Pierre Gouthière (born Bar-sur-
Aube 1732, died Paris 1813/4)
Red jasper and gilt bronze; 48 cm
high; *c*1775

The jasper, used in imitation of
antique porphyry, was brought
from Italy for the duc d'Aumont,
for whom Gouthière made this
piece. It passed from d'Aumont to
Marie-Antoinette, and was bought
by the fourth Marquess of Hertford
in 1865 (F292; gallery 22)

1

1

CUP AND SAUCER
Sèvres
Porcelain cup 9 cm high, saucer
15 cm diameter; 1766

The striking decoration was painted
by C-L Méreaud the younger. The
model may first have been designed
for Madame de Pompadour. Bought
by the third Marquess of Hertford
(C443; gallery 14)

2

VASE AND COVER (*vase à jet d'eau*)
Sèvres
Porcelain, 35 cm high; *c*1766

One of a pair; the dolphins were
probably introduced to mark the
future Louis XVI becoming
Dauphin in 1765. Bought by the
fourth Marquess of Hertford before
1865 (C284; gallery 14)

1

2

3

3

VASE AND COVER (*vase grec à
rosettes*)
Sèvres
Porcelain, 48.5 cm high; 1765

The model and title reflect the neo-
classical ideas then appearing in
French architecture and furniture.
This type of Greek key pattern first
appeared at the Sèvres factory
*c*1763 (C272; gallery 14)

4

6

5

4

VASE AND COVER (*vase E de 1780*)
Sèvres
Porcelain, 24 cm high; 1781

The decorative scene is copied from
Boucher's *Pygmalion and Galatea*.
From a garniture presented by
Louis XVI to Prince Henry of
Prussia in 1784. Bought by the
fourth Marquess of Hertford in
1860 (C334; gallery 12)

5

VASE (*vase feuille de myrte*)
Sèvres
Porcelain, 31.5 cm high; 1777

The basket of fruit was painted by
Vincent Taillandier and the
pointillé background by his wife
Geneviève (C296; gallery 2)

6

ICE-CREAM COOLER
Sèvres
Porcelain, 24 cm high; 1778

Part of the very large and
celebrated service commissioned
from the Sèvres factory by the
Empress Catherine II of Russia,
delivered to St Petersburg in 1779.
It was distinguished by its classical
shapes and decoration, on which
the Empress had insisted. This
piece was amongst the 160 looted
from the Hermitage Palace in 1837,
and was bought by the fourth
Marquess of Hertford in 1856-57
(C478; gallery 12)

DROP-FRONT SECRETAIRE
Probably by **Bernard Molitor** (born
Betzdorf 1755, died Paris 1810)
Oak veneered with mahogany,
boxwood, sycamore and ebony, the
top of Carrara marble; 139 cm high;
c1789

At the end of the 1780s, Molitor,
like Riesener, used carefully chosen
mahogany veneers to contrast with
elaborate gilt-bronze mounts (F309;
gallery 1)

110

1

DROP-FRONT SECRETAIRE
Jean-Henri Riesener (born 1734, died Paris 1806)
Oak veneered with holly, satiné and purplewood, with gilt-bronze mounts and top of Carrara marble, 139 cm high; 1783

Made for Marie-Antoinette for the Petit Trianon, this piece was delivered in 1783. The distinctive lozenge-shaped marquetry and the very fine mounts were in a style particularly favoured by the Queen. Bought by the fourth Marquess of Hertford in 1868 (F302; gallery 21)

2
DROP-FRONT SECRETAIRE, detail

1

2

1

COMBINED WORK, WRITING AND
READING TABLE

Martin Carlin (active 1766-85)
Veneered on oak with tulipwood,
with gilt-bronze mounts and set
with Sèvres porcelain plaques;
79 cm high (closed); 1783

The Sèvres plaques are dated 1783,
only two years before Carlin's
death. The intricate mechanism
allows the top to be raised for
reading; two candle stands pull out
at the sides, and there are two
drawers concealed behind the drop
front. Bought by the fourth
Marquess of Hertford in 1869
(F327, C506; gallery 25)

2

WORK TABLE

Adam Weisweiler (born Neuwied
*c*1750, died Paris after 1810)
Oak veneered with satinwood,
tulipwood, ebony and Wedgwood
plaques, with gilt-bronze mounts;
74 cm high; *c*1786-89

This piece was in the Tuileries in
1807 in the Empress Josephine's
appartements. The Wedgwood
plaques would have been imported
from England. Acquired by the
fourth Marquess of Hertford before
1865 (F325; gallery 23)

3

TOILET TABLE, detail of top

4

TOILET TABLE

Bernard Molitor (born Betzdorf
1755, died Paris 1810)
Oak veneered with elaborate
marquetry in purplewood,
satinwood, pear, sycamore, ebony
and others; 81 cm high; *c*1787-90

In the centre of the top is a marine
shell within a simulated marquetry
box, a usage also common in
contemporary English marquetry
(F321; gallery 23)

3

4

1

1

A BOY AS PIERROT
Jean-Honoré Fragonard (born
Grasse 1732, died Paris 1806)
Canvas, 60 × 50 cm; c1776-80

The fanciful composition imitates
several miniatures which have been
attributed to Fragonard, whose wife
exhibited a number of miniatures
of children between 1779 and 1782.
Bought by Sir Richard Wallace in
1872 as a Boucher (P412; gallery
25)

2

THE PAINTER'S FAMILY
Pierre-Adolf Hall (born Bôras
1739, died Liège 1793)
Ivory, 9 × 11 cm; 1776

Long recognised as one of Hall's
masterpieces, this miniature
demonstrates his easy grace and
fluent technique. Bought by Sir
Richard Wallace in 1872 (M186;
gallery 21)

3

THE PAINTER'S DAUGHTER, ADELAIDE
VICTORINE
Pierre-Adolf Hall (born Bôras
1739, died Liège 1793)
Ivory, 11 × 9 cm; c1785

The sitter was thirteen in 1785; she
is seen as a baby in *The painter's
family*. Bought by the fourth
Marquess of Hertford in 1864
(M189; gallery 21)

4
MARGUERITE GERARD
François Dumont (born Lunéville
1751, died Paris 1831)
Ivory, 16 × 12 cm; 1793

Marguerite Gérard was the pupil
and sister-in-law of Fragonard
whom she sometimes assisted with
his later paintings (M101;
gallery 21)

4

5

6

5
LADY HAMILTON AS A BACCHANTE
Henry Bone (born Truro 1755, died
London 1834)
Enamel on copper, 22 × 28 cm;
1803

Copied from a painting by Vigée Le
Brun, this miniature was once in
the collection of Sir William
Hamilton. Bought by the fourth
Marquess of Hertford in 1859
(M21; gallery 1)

6
GEORGIANA, DUCHESS OF DEVONSHIRE,
WITH LADY ELIZABETH FOSTER
Jean-Urbain Guérin (born
Strasbourg 1761, died Obernay
1836)
Ivory, 9.5 × 7 cm; c1791

Lady Elizabeth Foster was to
succeed Georgiana as Duchess of
Devonshire. Guérin, who painted
their portraits at Passy in 1791,
conceived this miniature in the
form of an antique cameo (M177;
gallery 21)

MADAME PERREGAUX
Elisabeth Vigée Le Brun (born
Paris 1755, died Paris 1842)
Panel, 100 × 79 cm; 1789

Madame Perregaux was the wife of
a Parisian banker whose clients
included the third Marquess of
Hertford and the artist herself.
Bought by the fourth Marquess of
Hertford in 1862 (P457; gallery 25)

MADAME DE SERILLY
Jean-Antoine Houdon (born
Versailles 1741, died Paris 1828)
Marble, 62 cm high; 1782

Madame de Sérilly was eighteen
when this bust was made. Seven
years later, she escaped the
guillotine only by alleging
pregnancy. The panelling from her
Parisian boudoir is preserved in the
Victoria and Albert Museum.
Bought by the fourth Marquess of
Hertford in 1865 (S26; gallery 25)

1

INNOCENCE

Jean-Baptiste Greuze (born
Tournus 1725, died Paris 1805)
Panel, 63 × 53 cm; *c*1790

The fourth Marquess of Hertford's
admiration of Greuze's sentimental
heads now seems almost
indiscriminate; he bought *Innocence*
in 1865 and it was one of his most
expensive purchases (P384;
gallery 23)

2

SOFA

Georges Jacob (born Cheny 1739,
died Paris 1814)
Mahogany with upholstery of
Beauvais tapestry, 229 cm wide;
*c*1780

From a set of two sofas and six
armchairs in the Wallace
Collection. The tapestry, of
*c*1755-60 and based on designs by
Oudry, was applied in the early
19th century (F191; gallery 24)

1

2

3

3

THE SLEEP OF VENUS AND CUPID
Marie-Constance Mayer (born
Paris 1775, died Paris 1821)
Canvas, 97 × 145 cm; 1806

This painting follows a drawing by
Prud'hon, Mayer's teacher and
companion; it belonged to the
Empress Josephine at Malmaison
before being bought by the fourth
Marquess of Hertford in 1866
(P348; gallery 21)

4

THE FOUNTAIN OF LOVE
Jean-Honoré Fragonard (born
Grasse 1732, died Paris 1806)
Canvas, 64 × 51 cm; 1785

The melting chiaroscuro and
classical figures contrast with
Fragonard's earlier cheerful
informality and anticipate the
classicism which came to dominate
French painting in the 1790s.
Bought by the fourth Marquess of
Hertford in 1870 (P394; gallery 21)

4

The Nineteenth Century

The nineteenth-century pictures in the Wallace Collection were nearly all acquired by the fourth Marquess of Hertford. Although he lived in Paris through one of the most eventful periods of French painting, from 1830 to 1870, his purchases were not adventurous, and reflected more the taste of a regular visitor to the annual *Salon*. Lord Hertford belonged to the great Romantic generation of Delacroix, Berlioz, Balzac and Hugo, but, where they expressed a fire in the soul, he was content with a gentler sentimentality. Apart from landscapes, his modern pictures showed scenes from the past, historical or literary, or exotic Oriental subjects whose actuality was incidental. He seldom commissioned works (the little Meissonier of *Napoleon and his staff officers* is a rare instance) and he bought his best-known nineteenth-century pictures, such as Delacroix's *Marino Faliero*, Vernet's *Dog of the Regiment* and *Wounded trumpeter*, and Delaroche's *Mazarin* and *Richelieu*, after their reputations had become well established.

An outstanding element of his modern collection was the number of works by Bonington. Eleven oils and twenty-five watercolours remain in the Wallace Collection, the richest public showing of his work. Bonington appealed to many of Hertford's predilections – pleasing subjects, warm colouring, and rich imagination – and with his adventurous technique he combined a sense of tradition, frequently acknowledging Dutch and Venetian masters of the past. Like Lord Hertford, Bonington was Anglo-French; born in Nottingham, he studied at the Ecole des Beaux-Arts in Paris and went on to exert a considerable influence on the course of French Romantic painting. Delacroix, a great admirer of his work and a close friend, once sketched with him in London, where they saw the Meyrick collection of armour, now in the Wallace Collection (see ARMS AND ARMOUR), and after this visit they had briefly shared a Paris studio. Delacroix was then painting his *Marino Faliero*, which Lord Hertford rather surprisingly acquired at the end of his life, despite the violence of the theme and the bold originality of the composition.

Both Bonington and Delacroix had cultivated subjects from past history which they reconstructed with a romantic attention to sentimental detail and character. They were avid readers of Scott, Byron, Shakespeare and of less well remembered authors like Dumesnil, from whom Bonington took the subject of his *Henri III*. Lord Hertford, who shared their romantic disposition, once began to translate Harrison Ainsworth's historical romance *Rookwood* into French. He clearly enjoyed historical tableaux, like the once famous Delaroches of *Mazarin* and *Richelieu*, for which he had to pay a heavy price in 1865, or baron Leys's *Frans Floris*, a careful reconstruction of sixteenth-century Antwerp.

There is a strong Napoleonic element running through Lord Hertford's collection. As a boy he had known many of Napoleon's officers who frequented his mother's home in Paris, and later his friendship with Napoleon III was founded, at least in part, on a shared admiration of Napoleon Bonaparte and his legend. The Wallace Collection retains a wealth of contemporary Napoleonic miniatures, such as *The Empress Josephine* and *Prince August* by J-B Isabey, but the principal illustrator of the Napoleonic legend was Horace Vernet whom Lord Hertford had known well. He bought a great quantity of his work, though rarely direct from the artist, including a group of his Napoleonic subjects painted between 1819 and 1823 when Louis XVIII was attempting to restore the credibility of the French monarchy. Vernet's pictures then caused alarm in Royalist circles and were banned from the *Salon*. The *Wounded trumpeter* and the *Dog of the Regiment*, according to contemporary accounts, became familiar throughout Europe through engravings, though now, when the ideology has ceased to matter, the appeal of their sentimental subjects hardly overcomes a pedestrian technique.

In his later years Vernet turned to Oriental subjects which equally appealed to Lord Hertford. He had once been attached to the British Consulate in Constantinople, and his addiction to Oriental armour has already been noticed (see ARMS AND ARMOUR). *The Turkish patrol* by Decamps, painted only three years after Lord Hertford's diplomatic excursion, shows a somewhat mischievous view of Ottoman administration in Smyrna. It verges on caricature, and was greatly admired as such by Heine at the 1831 Paris *Salon*. Lord Hertford's other Oriental scenes by Decamps, Marilhat and Vernet are rather less opinionated.

The finest of the few English nineteenth-century pictures is undoubtedly Lawrence's vivid portrait of *The Countess of Blessington*, the romantic characterization which, it was said, 'set all London raving'. The portrait was certainly acquired for personal reasons, since Lord Hertford had known Lady Blessington and indeed was supposed to have first met Napoleon III at Gore House, her London home. More curious is his purchase of Sully's *Queen Victoria* in 1855, immediately before the Queen's visit to Paris, where Lord Hertford was part of the Emperor's *comité d'honneur*.

Landseer's *Arab tent* was bought by Sir Richard Wallace after the death of his father, who had rather admired Landseer except when he painted scenes showing 'blood over all the animals'. The acquisition was to some extent diplomatic, for it was purchased from the Prince of Wales, who was not known for his thrift, for a sum in excess of 7,000 guineas. Wallace was to repeat such largesse when he bought Lawrence's portrait of George IV from the Duke of Teck in 1883 for £600, on the understanding, as he told the Duchess, that the picture would remain at her disposal whenever she wished to have it back.

QUEEN VICTORIA
Thomas Sully (born Horncastle
1783, died Philadelphia 1872)
Canvas, 143 × 113 cm; 1838

A reduced version of a whole-length
portrait of the young Queen at the
time of her Coronation which was
painted in London for the Society
of the Sons of St George of
Philadelphia. Bought by the fourth
Marquess of Hertford in 1855
(P564; gallery 1)

THE EXECUTION OF DOGE MARINO
FALIERO
Ferdinand-Victor-Eugène
Delacroix (born Paris 1798, died
Paris 1863)
Canvas, 146 × 114 cm; 1825-26

This dramatic composition
illustrates a scene from *Marino
Faliero*, the historical tragedy by
Byron set in 14th-century Venice. It
was painted during the time
Bonington shared Delacroix's Paris
studio. Bought by the fourth
Marquess of Hertford in 1868
(P282; gallery 20)

1

ON THE COAST OF PICARDY
Richard Parkes Bonington (born Nottingham 1802, died London 1828)
Canvas, 37 × 51 cm; 1826

One of Bonington's most accomplished French coast scenes, this was bought direct from the artist by the Duke of Bedford, from whose widow it was bought by the fourth Marquess of Hertford in 1853 (P341; gallery 10)

2

HENRI III
Richard Parkes Bonington (born Nottingham 1802, died London 1828)
Canvas, 54 × 64 cm; 1827-28

A study of the foppish character of the last Valois king of France, revealing Bonington's great affection for history and romance; he found the subject in a novel by Dumesnil published in 1825. Bought by the fourth Marquess of Hertford in 1860 (P323; gallery 10)

1

2

1

1

ROUEN

Richard Parkes Bonington (born Nottingham 1802, died London 1828)
Watercolour, 18 × 23.5 cm; 1825

Bought by the fourth Marquess of Hertford in 1843 (P704; ground floor corridor)

2

SUNSET IN THE PAYS DE CAUX

Richard Parkes Bonington (born Nottingham 1802, died London 1828)
Watercolour, 20 × 26 cm; 1828

Bought by the fourth Marquess of Hertford in 1863 (P708; ground floor corridor)

3

A VENETIAN SCENE

Richard Parkes Bonington (born Nottingham 1802, died London 1828)
Watercolour, 18 × 25 cm; c1828

Bought by the fourth Marquess of Hertford in 1846 (P674; ground floor corridor)

The fourth Marquess of Hertford was a great admirer of Bonington's work. These three watercolours, selected from the twenty-five in the Wallace Collection, demonstrate the richness of his technique and show how closely he matched Turner's achievement at this time

2

3

MARGARET, COUNTESS OF BLESSINGTON
Thomas Lawrence (born Bristol
1769, died London 1830)
Canvas, 91 × 67 cm; 1822

Famed for her looks and
accomplishments, Lady Blessington
presided over a literary salon at

Gore House, Kensington. This
portrait, said to be one of
Lawrence's finest characterizations,
was bought by the fourth Marquess
of Hertford at the Gore House sale
in 1849 (P558; gallery 1)

1

FRANS FLORIS GOING TO A SAINT
LUKE'S DAY FEAST 1540
Jan August Hendrik Leys (born
Antwerp 1815, died Antwerp 1869)
Panel, 66 × 90 cm; 1853

A celebrated Antwerp painter in his
day, Leys here paid deliberate
homage to a great Antwerp painter
of the past. Bought by the fourth
Marquess of Hertford in 1863
(P275; gallery 3)

2

CARDINAL MAZARIN'S LAST SICKNESS
Hippolyte (Paul) Delaroche (born
Paris 1797, died Paris 1856)
Canvas, 57 × 97 cm; 1830
(P314; gallery 10)

3

THE STATE BARGE OF CARDINAL
RICHELIEU ON THE RHONE
Hippolyte (Paul) Delaroche (born
Paris 1797, died Paris 1856)
Canvas, 56 × 97 cm; 1829
(P320; gallery 10)

Illustrating the contrasting last days
of the two great French Cardinals,
Mazarin eager for wealth, Richelieu
thirsting for revenge, these once
famous pictures were bought by the
fourth Marquess of Hertford in
1865.

4

THE DOG OF THE REGIMENT WOUNDED
Emile-Jean-Horace Vernet (born
Paris 1789, died Paris 1863)
Canvas, 53 × 64 cm; 1819
(P607; gallery 20)

5

THE WOUNDED TRUMPETER
Emile-Jean-Horace Vernet (born
Paris 1789, died Paris 1863)
Canvas, 53 × 64 cm; 1819
(P613; gallery 20)

These two paintings illustrating
scenes remembered from the
Napoleonic wars enjoyed a huge
reputation in the earlier 19th
century. They were bought by the
fourth Marquess of Hertford in
1865.

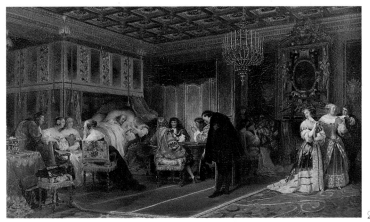

1

2

3

6

NAPOLEON AND HIS STAFF
Jean-Louis-Ernest Meissonier
(born Lyon 1815, died Paris 1891)
Panel, 17 × 18 cm; 1868

Commissioned by the fourth
Marquess of Hertford who insisted
on the insertion of Napoleon's
mameluke with his red and white
cap in the background (P290;
gallery 20)

4

5

6

7

8

127

FRANCESCA DA RIMINI
Ary Scheffer (born Dordrecht 1798, died Paris 1858)
Canvas, 167 × 234 cm; 1835

Illustrating a famous episode from the fifth canto of Dante's *Inferno*, in which Dante and Virgil see Paolo and Francesca condemned to the darkness of Hell with the souls of the lustful. This is the prime version of a composition Scheffer repeated several times and it has a frame which he specially devised to suit the subject. Bought by the fourth Marquess of Hertford in 1870 (P316; gallery 20)

1
THE ARAB TENT
Edwin Henry Landseer (born London 1802, died London 1873)
Canvas, 154 × 226 cm; 1866

Bought from the artist by the Prince of Wales who sold it to Sir Richard Wallace in 1878 for 7,440 guineas, the highest price paid for any of the pictures in the Wallace Collection (P376; gallery 9)

2
THE TURKISH PATROL
Alexandre-Gabriel Decamps (born Paris 1803, died Fontainebleau 1860)
Canvas, 115 × 179 cm; 1831

Decamps' first major painting of an Oriental subject, this was based on his observation of the Cadji-Bey (chief of police) at Smyrna in 1828. Bought by the fourth Marquess of Hertford in 1855 (P307; gallery 8)

1

2

Plan of the Galleries

The numbers refer to the galleries. All illustrations have numbers that refer to this plan.

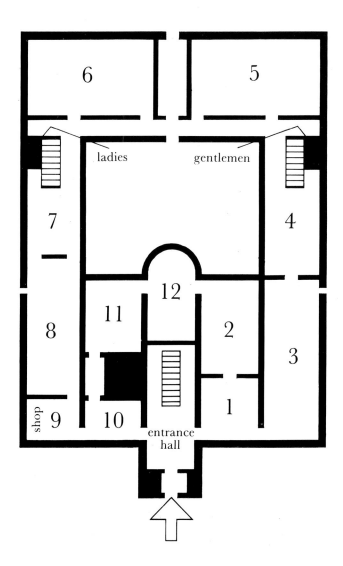

Ground floor

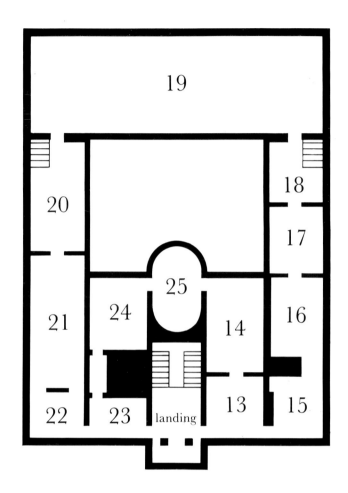

First floor

Index of colour plates